PRAISE FOR PEAK MINDSET

Peak Mindset has helped me more than I can put into words. This book is one of a kind; it explains everything in the simplest way possible by giving examples and telling a story. There is no way anyone who reads this goes away without learning something.

— Readers' Favourite

A short, accessibly written, self-help book in which the author attempts to help us to find happiness.

— Wishing Shelf

PEAK MINDSET

APPLY REALISTIC THINKING WHEN STUDIES
ON HAPPINESS FAIL TO MAKE US HAPPY

SAID HASYIM

Edited by
DAVID ARETHA

For You

Don't expect light at the end of the tunnel;

find the lightened tunnel to go through.

CONTENTS

DISCLAIMER

This book contains advice and information relating to health care. It should be used to supplement rather than replace the advice of your doctor or another trained health professional. If you know or suspect you have a health problem, it is recommended that you seek your physician's advice before embarking on any medical program or treatment. All efforts have been made to assure the accuracy of the information contained in this book as of the date of publication. The author disclaims liability for any medical outcomes that may occur as a result of applying the methods suggested in this book.

INTRODUCTION

Every decision you make now paves a path toward a better or worse version of your future self. Every action you take leads you closer to or further from your goals. Your mindset is the guiding star that directs what you will do in life.

Jack was a hardworking stockbroker. After working for over twenty years in a renowned investment brokerage firm, he climbed the corporate ladder and took a senior position. Jack did not really like his job, and from time to time, he experienced stress from its rigorous demands. However, the pay was high. That was what kept him in the company for so long. After all, he couldn't be sure he could get another job with so great a salary.

Now, in his sixties, he has accumulated enough wealth to retire comfortably and has left the workforce. Despite that, he does not feel fulfilled. He remembers not spending a lot of time with his children since he had to spend more time in his cubicle. He missed his "moment" with his children—they are grown up now and not very close to him. Pretty sad. "But that's to be expected from children nowadays," he mutters to himself.

He once dreamed of traveling to Alaska and living in the wild for a few days, but now he is too old for that. Besides, his doctor has prohibited him from cold-weather travel because of his high risk of hypothermia. He retires rich but not delighted with his life.

Johnny worked in the same investment company as Jack. Johnny too was overwhelmed by the work and did not enjoy the spreadsheets nor the stress of corporate culture. He wished to move back to his rural hometown and make a living by farming. But strapped for funds, he knew he needed to continue working for the time being. He started learning about agricultural systems on the weekends. By the time he had enough capital to leave the company, he had amassed a lot of agricultural knowledge.

And so, the summer after he quit his job, he made a pilgrimage to his old village to start his own farm. Despite the exhausting workload, he enjoyed his farming life and couldn't wait to wake up every morning to watch his piglets frolic in a pasture and his hens lay eggs and to harvest ripe tomatoes. Despite not earning as high an income as when he was in the investment company, he enjoyed the freedom of using his time as he wished. He even made time to visit Spain to savor his favorite *jamón ibérico* with his family.

After ten years of getting caked with soil and sweat daily, he developed a successful farm that now enables him to export his produce worldwide and has landed him multiple big restaurant accounts. He earns a much higher income now than he would have thought possible as a farmer. Still spry in his sixties, he continues working on his farm and has a lot of fun with his grandchildren. When asked what makes him happy, he says, "The ability to rear my goats, milk my cows, collect eggs, and transplant seedlings. These are my sources of joy and the only things keeping me together. I couldn't imagine living otherwise."

Jack and Johnny started at the same spot but ended up with vastly different outcomes and happiness levels. One adopted a mindset that maximized his potential to prioritize long-term happiness, while the other hinged his happiness on life's chance circumstances.

I myself have trained and adopted a mindset that allows me to realistically achieve most of the things that I want in life—including things that I never thought I could possibly do—to progress as much as I want to in both my personal and professional lives and to be as productive as I can. Now I wish to share my findings with you. They have benefitted me, and I hope they do the same for you.

In this book, I will cover how to use your subconscious mind—the most powerful part of your mind, which guides your life decisions and actions. I will also show you how to handle daily stress and adopt a mindset that will minimize future unhappiness while helping you inch closer to your goals day by day. I will unravel commonly believed misconceptions on stress cures and happiness to help you develop realistic thinking while pursuing your dreams.

1
___

THE SUBCONSCIOUSNESS

 Just have a little faith.

— MICHAEL SCOFIELD, *PRISON BREAK*

BENEATH OUR CONSCIOUS MIND LIES OUR SUBCONSCIOUS. IT stores every desire, thought, and belief you hold. Experiencing gut feelings, hunches, an inner voice, instincts, a sixth sense, and intuition are your subconsciousness in action.

A team of firefighters in Chicago, Illinois, went into a living room to extinguish a fire in a kitchen. Strangely, though, the fire would not go out. One firefighter had an uneasy feeling and ordered everyone to get out of the house. Shortly afterward, the living room floor where they had stood collapsed.

When the firefighter was asked how he knew the floor would collapse, he said he didn't know. His gut feeling had told him something was not right. His subconsciousness that had been collecting a lifetime of experience saved his and his teammates' lives.

Although you may not realize it, your behavior, thoughts, judgments, preferences, and feelings are governed by your subconsciousness. You may meet someone new and for no reason feel strongly connected to them. Perhaps they said something or behave in some way that your subconsciousness recognizes as friendliness or closeness. Likewise, you may meet someone and instantly feel something is not right, although you just can't reason it out.

While your conscious mind can be seen as the commander of your being, your subconscious mind can be seen as the soldiers. Your conscious mind gives an order, and your subconscious mind carries it out without discriminating whether the order is good or bad or real or imagined.[1] Your conscious mind is your subjective mind, while your subconscious mind is your objective mind.

Any belief, regardless of whether it is true or false, held by you influences you to act as if it is the truth. If I tell you that Jack cannot be trusted, without evaluating the accuracy of my statement, you will begin to distance yourself from Jack and treat him as a cagey person. You will not want to open up to Jack and will refuse to smile at him. In reciprocation, Jack notices your inability to trust him and thinks you are malevolent. Your body language says it loud and clear. Jack begins to stay away and avoids sharing personal information with you. You now witness that Jack is not to be trusted. Your expectation becomes a somber premonition.

Listening to a pre-war speech raises the build-up of energy in your body. Even a single word can influence your subconsciousness. Social psychologist John Bargh conducted an experiment in 1996.[2] Participants who were shown the word "elderly" walked slowly compared to others who were shown other words. You have no awareness of this process happening because it lies within your subconscious level.

Your subconscious mind could turn a fairly neutral situation into a calamity. When it sees a negative statement as the truth, it carries on as if that statement is fact and will sometimes turn it into reality by bringing on hindrances, delays, and excuses. What if you could reverse this phenomenon and use this psychological effect on yourself positively? You can certainly create a far more pleasing outcome. Let's exploit your subconscious power to your advantage and bring out the best in you.

How Does the Subconscious Mind Work?

Your subconsciousness relies on your consciousness to process messages.

- When your conscious mind desires something badly enough, your subconscious mind knows it and will muster your resources to see that wish fulfilled.
- When your conscious mind believes in something genuinely—even if it is not the truth—your subconscious mind responds to the belief and will spur you to act as if it is the truth.
- When your conscious mind thinks negatively, your

subconscious mind accepts those thoughts and keeps you living negatively.

Imagine that you are at work and your colleague tells you that you look sick. Your subconsciousness lets that message sink in, and suddenly, the blood vessels in your face constrict, making your face turn pale. Now, you look really sick, even though you aren't.[3] If your consciousness believes a message, your gullible subconsciousness will believe it. If your consciousness doesn't believe a message given to you, however, the message does not affect you. For example, if you tell an experienced pilot that he looks like he has airsickness, he will probably laugh at you.

Humans are influenced by what they want to believe.[4] If you want to believe a fact, it is hard for others to make you believe otherwise, even when the truth is obvious. If you want to believe an interviewee is qualified, a few questions answered correctly are enough, but when you don't want to believe that interviewee is qualified, you may request proof of past jobs, a lot of evidence of their abilities, and recommendation letters. Those, too, may not yet satisfy you.

A convincing fortune-teller can change their clients' futures for the better or worse. In 1989, a Belgian man named Max went to see a fortune-teller who ended up telling him that he would die of an air attack. He believed the prediction and took sick leave from his work to shut himself in his house to avoid any plane. An unmanned MiG-23M fighter plane ran out of fuel and fell onto Max's house, killing him in the process. The prediction of his death became true. Sadly, the innocent fortune-teller had been just trying to make a living with no intention of *killing* the unwary client using a false story.

Now, imagine you are feeling miserable and lonely, and a fortune-teller tells you that you will be surrounded by many good friends in the next three months. Your mood and spirit are lifted. You become more open to new people. You socialize and talk more with strangers. You are happier than you were. People become attracted to you. During the next three months, you end up with several good friends because of your behavioral changes.

Religious healing rituals have miraculously healed the sick. In many of those cases, the sick manifested unfettered faith that the ritual would fix them, and then they were fixed. The ritual did not fix them; their own subconscious minds perceived that the ritual was effective, so it seemed to be. Blessed are people who are faithfully guided by positive religious practices.

Tetraphobia, the fear of the number four, is most prevalent among Asians. Most Asians have long held a superstition that the number four represents death because *four* is a homophone of *death* in Chinese and Japanese. A study published in 2001 found that the mortality rate of Chinese and Japanese Americans from chronic heart disease is the highest on the fourth of each month.[5] The association of the number *four* with *death* becomes reality.

If a strong positive belief can heal your body or reorient all aspects of your life for the better, there is no reason not to apply this principle to speeding up your progress in life. Likewise, the reverse, self-doubting, undercuts your performance.[6]

Mental Attitude

One morning, Mr. Pessimistic saw a job opening in a newspaper and found his dream job. He felt applying would be futile because he wouldn't be chosen. After all, he had failed many times in the past. He was convinced that he would fail again this time. Therefore, he didn't bother applying for the job.

Mr. Optimistic saw the same ad that morning too. Feeling positive, he applied for the job straight away, thinking that he would definitely be chosen. He went for the interview. He was rejected, but at least he took his chance. Good try. Better luck next time.

Mr. Realistic saw the ad for his dream job. He read all the requirements and found that he fulfilled all the qualifications since he has been working to prepare for his ideal job for months. He had known he was inept at accounting, so he spent an extensive amount of time taking an accounting class. Now there was a job opening, and he was ready for it. The interview went well, and he could answer all the test questions accurately.

These three men have the same intelligence but different mental attitudes. They lead different types of lives, and it does not take much to guess that Mr. Realistic had the highest chance of succeeding. Optimists who take chances are better off than pessimists who let things pass them by. Best of all, realists fix their weaknesses to increase their likelihood of success before taking chances.

All the messages your subconsciousness receives invariably reside in your mental attitude. Your mental attitude has the highest influence on your subconsciousness because the thoughts and beliefs that you communicate to your subconsciousness are derived from your mental attitude, which sticks with you 24/7. Pessimists think negatively all the time. Optimists think positively all the time. Realists think both positively and negatively.

PESSIMISTIC

If you plant thoughts of happiness, success, optimism, and peace in your mindset, you will react and behave in accordance with those thoughts.

- Harbor negative thoughts, and you will always want to stay away from any new endeavor, stifle your own creativity, and won't enjoy your life fully.
- Harbor positive thoughts, and you will always be ready to welcome new challenges, feel more alive, and see the world as beautiful.

THE MENTAL CHATTER in the head of pessimists is all about negativity, from the time they wake up to the time they go to sleep. Pessimists hold the belief that they will always fail every day. That is a serious belief that their subconsciousness has deeply accepted. This attitude is so destructive that the subconsciousness discredits any effort and does not want any progress at all. No action equals zero opportunity.

Negative thoughts poison your brain plasticity. Your brain learns to see every situation negatively, and that gets reflected in your behavior and attitude daily. If you are pessimistic about life and always carry around mental chatter like this every day: "It will not work," "It is too difficult," "The time is not right yet," and "I'm not qualified to do this," you will not go very far. Remember that your subconsciousness does not judge the truthfulness of your mental statements. If you accept a statement, it accepts it. Your subconsciousness will execute your orders and always lead you away from opportunities for success because the path to it is seen as full of threats. Staying in your comfort zone becomes the safest way.

Note: Brain plasticity is the ability of your brain to change based on the stimuli fed to it from your environment, thoughts, and actions.

OPTIMISTIC

OPTIMISTS ALWAYS THINK POSITIVELY and have set up a great deal of positive fruition in their minds. They fare better than the negative thinkers. However, despite having all the advantages their positive subconsciousness mind can provide, they lack personal assessment of their drawbacks. They think that if they don't get what they want, it is because they didn't desire it badly enough.

- "If you don't win the championship, it is simply because you don't desire it badly enough." Who does not want to win badly enough? It is not a competition of desire but a competition of preparation.

- "If you are poor, it is because you don't desire to be rich." Who does not want to get out of poverty? Having a desire alone will not make you rich.

A strong desire in your subconscious mind cannot replace sweat and work. Simply desiring what you want is not enough. Your subconscious mind cannot magically transform any external goal you wish for into reality. It cannot make you have more money, be healthier, or get into a better relationship in an instant. You can't just fire off some desire and expect it to come true. That is wishful thinking. Strictly relying on the desire to have your wishes granted discourages you from making any plan to see them happen and genuinely assessing your weaknesses. Having a desire without action is futile. You can't gain success in any corner if you're not willing to prepare for it. If you aren't ready to get there yet, accept that and improve instead of just positively thinking that you can do anything, even without preparing first.

Our brains are already prone to overestimating our abilities. We tend to overestimate our likelihood of encountering positive events. We overestimate our life expectancy, our children's abilities, and our success.[7] This tendency is called optimism bias. Thus, optimistic thinkers have higher risks of grandiosity and of becoming so overconfident that they don't find it necessary to prepare for or work toward anything. Excessively optimistic people have an increased risk of depression when they don't get what they want.

Realistic

Realists take their chances on ventures they know they are good at but also skip opportunities they know they are underprepared for. This attitude is not inherently bad, but it dismisses pursuing anything that is beyond their current capacity. The expected goal is limited by the ceiling capacity that realists fastidiously think they have.

This is good, but not great. What separates the great from the good is being realistic while utilizing the power of positive subconsciousness.

Honestly assess your strengths and weaknesses. Use the positive subconscious mind to stretch your capacity and increase your chance of success. Don't rely on dreaming to make things happen. Whether your goal will be fulfilled or not depends entirely on the rest of your actions and luck.

When your desire for success has sunk deep into your subconsciousness, the natural next step is to get your desire translated into concrete actions and focus all your resources on seeing it come true. Your creativity is ramped up toward reaching that goal. Coupling this benefit with a realistic mindset primes your brain to increase your determination and help you put together a concerted effort to prepare yourself for greater success.

- You begin to evaluate that your competition does not remain static even as you improve; they may beat you next time if you slack now.

- You begin to see your weaknesses that need improvement if you want your desire to be fulfilled.
- You begin to accept the sunk cost of the inferior results of your initial attempts and try again, getting better and better.

THE PRESENCE of positive subconsciousness keeps you persevering with your goal as long as there is at least a 1 percent chance of succeeding. Shift your mental attitude to "realistic" and use positive subconsciousness to your advantage to reach greater heights.

Stimulate Communication with Your Subconscious Mind

Tetris syndrome occurs when you play a video game for a prolonged period, causing your behavior and mental images to emulate what you do and see in the game. People who play the game Tetris for a long time, for example, begin to see the world's objects as falling boxes and attempt to make them fit together as they do in a Tetris game.[8] The same effect can be observed by playing other games too.

We will replicate the effect of Tetris syndrome in a productive way, not by playing video games but by using the appropriate practices to **send** messages into your subconsciousness and by adopting the right mindset to **re-enact** your subliminal messages.

The Practices

Apply the following practices to increase the chance of intentionally sending messages into your subconsciousness.

FAKE IT UNTIL YOU MAKE IT

USE your conscious mind to fake the idea that your physical appearance is whatever you envision it to be. Remember that your subconscious mind cannot discern truth from falsity. Your innocent subconsciousness will accept this idea as real. If you want your subconsciousness to believe in something, fake it until you make it.

- If you want to feel happy, fake your smile. Your subconscious mind acts on the "smile" cue, which tells it to feel happy.[9]
- If you want to feel confident, fake your confidence: Dress well, stand upright, and walk with confidence.[10] Your subconscious mind reads your posture and feels you are well-dressed. It accepts the fact that you look good and exude self-confidence.

VISUALIZATION

Visualization is a powerful tool that can override your logical thinking. Mentally practicing a musical instrument produces real improvement in performance as much as if it were practiced physically.[11] Visualizing tasty food makes you salivate. The same applies when you visualize a spooky figure as you are lying in your bed to sleep. It can feel so real that it can really seem like an imminent danger compared to how it feels when you don't visualize it. People with aphantasia cannot adopt this technique. That's why they are also immune to ghost stories.

Note: Aphantasia is the inability to construct mental images in one's mind.

Practice visualizing positivity daily to implant a powerful message in your subconsciousness. Visualize positive events as vividly as possible and make that belief indelible.

SELF-AFFIRMATION

To manipulate your subconsciousness to your benefits, you need to implant a positive belief—and it must be a truly firm belief—in your subconsciousness. Say to yourself what you desire to be true, such as:

> "I am happy."
> "I am progressing well in life."
> "I will complete my project successfully."

CERTAINLY, it is not easy to make these simple statements come true. You can practice believing "I will graduate with high distinction" every day, but it will still not work as long as you have a shadow of doubt about its accuracy. Your conscious mind is no fool and will recognize this fraudulence. It rejects the message before it has a chance to pass the command to the subconscious mind. Your conscious mind already knows that you are trying to believe a blatant lie. This is the reason most people fail in using this technique. It is indeed difficult because we still need to work around our conscious mind, which is aware when this deliberate attempt is used to trick the subconscious mind.

You may adopt the following to increase the chance of successfully bypassing your consciousness:

1. Use a realistic statement.

The sentence must be achievable and very close to the present truth to lower the chance of your consciousness perceiving the message as false. After all, you can only achieve your goal step by step. A farfetched statement also makes you lose sight of what preparation you can do to help reach your objective.

- You can't use "I will win a national championship" if you haven't been recruited for college basketball. Instead, use "I am skillful and a valuable player who will play college basketball."
- You can't use "I will be recruited for college basketball" if you haven't started any preparation. The appropriate choice would be: "My dribbling skill is improving every day."

Be specific in your sentence. Don't say, "I will succeed." That sentence is too general for your mind to act on and will bring some conflicts or arguments into your thought process because you cannot truly believe something that is not specific. As a result, you will do nothing about it. Instead, say "My violin practice improves every day," and your mind will urge you to start practicing violin with the intent to improve.

Don't use a weak sentence either. If you wish to be selected in an audition, you shouldn't tell your mind, "I wish to be selected," or "I hope to be selected." Your conscious mind knows that it is just a wish and not a belief. Instead, use a strong sentence that strengthens your belief. Say, "I will be selected at my *America's Got Talent* 2022 singing audition."

As you affirm your desire, close your eyes to visualize it happening and engage all your five senses—sight, touch, hearing, taste, and smell—or whichever of those will make your affirmation evocative. Visualize that you hear the cheers of the audience when the three judges in front of you announce that you have passed the audition as you grip the microphone in your hand and inhale the scents within the stadium.

It feels odd, but when you do it repeatedly, your conscious mind begins to perceive what you affirm as true—even if it is only partially true or not true at all—which then allows your subconscious mind to accept your statement.

By maintaining this practice daily, your subconsciousness keeps you focused on your desire and increases your motivation to follow your goal through to its realization.

2. Self-affirm when your consciousness is weakened.

To bring out a higher chance of success in sending any message to your subconsciousness, you must be in a state in which your consciousness is weakened. When your conscious mind is suppressed, it has less of a chance to interfere with and filter the truthfulness of the message you send to your subconscious mind.

A quick way to weaken your conscious mind is to get drunk. You can convince a drunkard easily that he is Napoleon Bonaparte, and he will believe it. Of course, we shouldn't abuse alcohol for the sake of communicating with our subconscious mind, lest we wither our brain cells and ruin our kidneys.

To condition your subconscious mind to readily accept your incoming message, self-affirm before you sleep. When you are sleepy, your consciousness capacity is lowered. It is a good time to inject messages into your subconsciousness. In an unconscious state, however, you won't be able to think straight to initiate any affirmation. The best time to do so is when you are sleepy and have not fully lost your consciousness, which is approximately the few minutes before you sleep. This is hard to predict unless you have a fixed sleeping time, in which case, your body's clock knows the exact time you will fall into slumber.

You will not be able to continuously send the intended message to your subconscious mind because when you finally get to sleep, you will lose control of your thoughts. Your mind may return to something you thought about earlier or wander down another rabbit hole entirely. If it continues replaying your message, however, you have a higher chance of getting it passed on to your subconscious mind.

The Mindsets

CULTIVATE THE FOLLOWING mindsets to re-enact the messages you have sent to your subconsciousness.

GROWTH MINDSET

AMERICAN PSYCHOLOGIST CAROL DWECK has conducted a lot of research to prove that people with a growth mindset progress much better in life than those with a fixed mindset.[12] People with growth mindsets believe they can continue to grow. The innate skills and intelligence that come at birth are corrigible. People with indwelling fixed mindsets hold on to the belief that intellectual abilities and skills are fixed at birth, and they are not changeable.

Carol Dweck and her colleagues conducted a study in 2007 to track the math grades of over three hundred students from the beginning of seventh grade to eighth grade.[13] These students were assessed on whether they had a growth mindset or fixed mindset. Students with growth mindsets viewed difficult math questions challenging, and the effort they exerted led to their improvement. When they didn't get a math answer right, they stayed motivated to improve. On the other hand, students with fixed mindsets preferred easy math questions, did not believe that the effort spent on hard questions led to any improvement, and found difficult math questions discouraging because they seemed beyond the students' talents.

At the end of eighth grade, the math grades of students with growth mindsets revealed consistent improvement, while that of students with fixed mindsets showed steady deterioration. The belief in their fixed abilities stymied development because it demotivated them from trying and improving.

If you have been led to believe that your abilities were given at birth, now you can dispose of that belief and switch your mindset to a growth mindset. You can absolutely improve your abilities, no matter what genes you were bestowed with. Adopting this mindset reinforces your messages to your subconsciousness that you are progressing.

Salvage from Failure

Faced with failure, your mind often focuses only on the loss and misses seeing any other available options. *That's it. I have failed*, you might think. This belief then stops you from taking any further action, and as a result, you stop improving. You give up. The worst part is, you can become afraid of moving on with your life.

- Breaking up with your fiancée could make you distrustful of any relationship.
- Failing a test could make you hate education forever.
- Losing a business could make you reluctant to venture into a new one.

"What doesn't kill you makes you stronger" only works if your mind believes it to be so. You can always salvage something out of your failure, with the right mindset. See failure as a part of your learning process, not the end of the world. A failure is just a short-term hiccup that must not stop your long-term goal. People who believe that a temporary failure is an opportunity to learn are more likely to grow.

- Jack Ma may not have founded an e-commerce titan if he hadn't been rejected from working for KFC.
- Jeff Bezos may not have founded Amazon if he hadn't been rejected from working for Intel.
- Warren Buffett may not have become massively successful in his investment career if he hadn't been rejected by Harvard Business School.

Having this mindset allows you to keep going despite even major failures. The desire to progress remains kindled in your subconscious mind and helps you take constructive steps to prevent future failure. Failing is expensive enough, but not learning from it and bringing something positive out of it makes it far more costly.

SUCCESS DOES NOT MEAN YOU ARE GOOD

TOO OFTEN, people who are highly educated or have succeeded previously elevate their optimism.[14] Their confidence level and risk-appetite soar. Their brain reduces their previous feelings of caution. And, understandably, the world rewards people who project confidence. High confidence is thought to equate to high competence, even though it can cause ineffective decision-making.

Just as you should salvage every benefit you can from your failure, so should you salvage the benefits from your successes. Ask why you succeeded and learn or capitalize on the reasons that allowed you to maintain your success.

- Did your competitor neglect to provide a complete submission, thus winning you the contest—which means you are not as talented as you think?
- Did your classmate not sleep well due to a work commitment, causing you to outscore him—which means you are not necessarily smarter than him?
- Did you make more sales just because your product is better—meaning you are not a better salesperson than your peers?

Reveling in your win without evaluating the reasons is short-sighted. Winning once does not mean it will happen next time. Whatever the situations that made you successful were, never let your mind lose sight of reality. You can fool others but not yourself. Only when you understand the reasons behind your achievements can you continue to progress.

Your Expectations

When you expect things to work out well, it becomes much more likely to happen. The term psychologists refer to as the Rosenthal effect states that high expectations lead to improved performance. A leader's high expectations of subordinates lead to those subordinates' high performance.[15] So, too, does a teacher's high expectations lead to a better performance among his or her students.

In a public elementary school experiment, a psychologist told teachers that certain students were expected to do very well in the future based on their results from a particular test, even though there was no actual test and those students were selected at random.[16] Over the next few months, the researchers observed the heightened expectations from the teachers for those selected students. The teachers were more engaged with the students' questions, gave more encouragement to the students, and attended to more questions from them. In the end, these randomly selected students produced better schoolwork and scored higher in examinations than those not selected. The teachers' expectations had bloomed into reality. The recipients subtly received the signal from their teacher, whether or not it was overtly mentioned to them. In effect, the expectations from the teachers transformed into reality. The recipients' minds perceived the message as the truth and set forth to make it happen.

Watch out for others who may tell you:

- "That's impossible to achieve."
- "Who are you to dream of that?"
- "You won't make it."
- "It's no use to try. Those people have better luck."

Reject these statements immediately. Don't believe them or let them sink into your subconsciousness. Never say any of these to your children, who are too naïve to comprehend the catastrophic effects these words can have on their subconsciousness.

You can also use this to help others fortify their desire. Set high but realistic expectations for your children, friends, or colleagues, and watch them move into high gear to meet those expectations.

Take the Positive Viewpoint

You are strongly affected by how you view all aspects of your life—your business, your home life, your relationships, etc. Your viewpoints can make or break your goals.

Two salesmen have the same job description, same pool of clients, and same skills but have different ways of thinking. One views his job as meaningful in that it allows him to change his clients' lives for the better, while the other views it as a means to get a paycheck. It is no surprise that the former is happier, makes more sales, and has a far greater chance of success than the latter. The former genuinely likes his clients and sees how his product can benefit them; his clients, in turn, trust and recommend him to their friends. The latter sees his clients as potential prey to profit from; his clients sense this from his aggressive body language and are inclined to keep their distance.

Try to see your life through the lens of positivity. If this feels challenging to you, at least at first, don't be too surprised. It is easy to conceive negative thoughts as we go through our daily lives. Take, for example, the following obstacles:

1. Brain plasticity molded by your occupation can impact your perspective.

MANY OCCUPATIONS, including those of analysts, lawyers, stockbrokers, and auditors, require that workers are good at spotting problems. After years of working in one of these positions, your brain reshapes and becomes good at looking for mistakes. You carry this fault-finding habit into other areas of your life and become adept at viewing life through the lens of negativity. In the long run, if this habit escalates, you can hurt your relationships with family members and others.

It is no wonder that lawyers are 3.6 times more likely to suffer from depression than those in other occupations.[17] They are constantly scanning for flaws and the next threat, which frequently triggers their fight-or-flight instinct. Their brain is trained to be critical, and it becomes prone to spotting mistakes, even those of their loved ones.

As a young graduate, I worked as an application consultant for a bank client for over two years. Looking for and preventing mistakes was an essential part of the job. Every transaction failure was treated as an emergency. It was common to get a nasty scolding whenever there was any failure. I was expected to be ready 24/7 whenever a problem occurred. Being accessible all the time caused my personal life's boundaries to collapse. The attitude I used at work spilled over into my personal life. I treated minor issues as if they were emergencies; I was always on the lookout for problems.

People who have been in hectic occupations for long periods of time are influenced by their jobs in the same way. It is also not easy for most to just leave their jobs to avoid this problem, and I don't intend to claim that it is possible to fix this problem without leaving your job. Your occupation shapes your brain. At best, you can alleviate (not eliminate) the fault-finding habit by intentionally rewiring your brain to counterbalance that habit using some techniques that we will discuss later.

2. Misfortune can drag down your perspective.

THE HUMAN BRAIN is prone to wallowing in negative thoughts during misfortune or a crisis. One example could be observed during the COVID-19 pandemic. Excluding the individuals who were the victims of the pandemic—my sincere prayers go out to them and their relatives—a great many people felt helpless, viewed this catastrophic event as the end of the world, and thought that they might lose their jobs at any time. Another group of people saw it differently. They saw that there was nothing they could do other than cooperate with the authorities to avoid further virus spread and prepare themselves for the bounce-back of the job market. Using this positive mindset, they felt blessed that they and their family members were still safe. Despite being locked down at home, they capitalized on their spare time to improve themselves by learning new crafts and forging deeper bonds with their family. Meanwhile, the former group was busy instilling fear in themselves by anxiously waiting for the daily news on the infected count or panicking about the possibility of essentials going out of stock. This group expected only doom while others were busy upgrading themselves.

When the pandemic was over, these positive people's thoughts blossomed into potent self-fulfilling prophesies. They came back better than they were before the crisis; the ones who dwelled on negative thoughts came back no better than they had been before or were even possibly worse. They lost over a year to worrying about things they couldn't control, time that could otherwise have been used productively.

When stricken with inevitable misfortune, don't just look at your situation with misery and despair. Instead, imagine how it could be worse, which will soften the emotional impact of the misfortune.

AS EXPLAINED ABOVE, negative thoughts paralyze creativity and progress and can lead to anxiety or even depression. The ones who embrace positive thoughts have a higher chance of winning. If your brain tends to see things negatively, this will only be disadvantageous for you. To be fair, once you're in a depressed state, it can be almost impossible for you to feel positive. The good news is, you can rewire your brain to prioritize seeing things positively.

Apply the following two techniques to help you focus on positive viewpoints even when faced with life's most daunting difficulties.

GRATITUDE JOURNALING

DAILY GRATITUDE JOURNALING rewires your brain to look for positivity. We feel grateful when we acknowledge the positivity we receive in life, but unfortunately, most of us take things for granted. Our consumption-based society further fuels our impossible-to-satisfy craving for things. Often, we only start to feel grateful for something after it's lost.

- Prisoners locked in a concentration camp can feel great joy from just watching a sunset.
- Having a full working limb would be a dream come true for an amputee.
- Clean air is a luxury for people living in Mali who experience dangerously high-level air pollution.

Gratitude journaling forces you to reminisce on what you already have rather than focusing on what you don't have. Gratitude journaling creates a sense of abundance. You will realize that most of what you are worrying about is minor compared to what you already have in life: shelter, friends, family, and achievements. Gratitude changes your perspective, enabling you to see the gift of life and that you already have more than enough.

- Be contented with what you own—you will not be so easily swayed by the impulse to buy more.
- When you are angry at your kids, you will be less likely

to be aggressive toward them if you remind yourself that they are a huge source of your joy.

- If you view the world optimistically, you can spot more opportunities instead of just seeing the gloomy part of life.

Amplify the effect of gratitude by imagining losing the things that you have. Humans have the propensity to experience losses more gravely than the equivalent gains. This cognitive bias is called loss aversion. Use this mind behaviour to your advantage. Think about how you will get through life if you lose your sight. Take a few minutes to undergo the hardship. As you complete the practice, you will feel the burst of bliss of still having what you have.

SELF-APPRECIATION

ANOTHER PRACTICE that increases positive awareness is self-appreciation. This focuses on rediscovering your positive personal qualities and appreciating them. Tell yourself:

- "I am self-motivated."
- "I love my family."
- "I am improving my craft."
- "I am prepared to succeed."
- "I am healthy and continue to observe healthy living."

PRACTICE GRATITUDE and self-appreciation journaling every day, recalling the good things—large or small—about your job, life, or family. As you get used to this, it will become easy for you to move intentionally toward a positive perspective in every situation, which, in turn, will lower your stress level and make you appreciate your life a little more.

For this to work in your favor, you must do it repetitively. Come up with one grateful and appreciative thought each day instead of brainstorming a list of a hundred new items to be grateful for in one day. Harnessing brain plasticity requires repetition, allowing you to mold your brain in the direction you want it to grow.

YOUR THOUGHTS directly influence your progress in life. Positive thoughts allow you to embrace new ideas, opportunities, and challenges. As your brain can only see things from one point of view at a time, help it to prioritize seeing the world through the lens of positivity.

Don't use positive thinking as an excuse to neglect your problems. Use it only to enhance your subconscious power in support of your goals. Remember to adopt a realistic mental attitude and acknowledge the risks in every opportunity and that plans don't always work as intended. Don't pretend everything is wonderful if it isn't or lie to yourself. While you continue to think positively, be realistic regarding what you can control and what you can't, and then plan and prepare instead of letting setbacks consume you or falling into the trap of feeling overconfident.

All the techniques I mentioned here are not new. You must have heard this advice before, but do you actually practice any of these techniques in your life? For a long time, I didn't because it all sounded too good to be true and too simple to produce any quality results, but then I learned the neuroscience behind it. If you don't practice these exercises yet, I hope you now have a good reason to do so. And now, you can do it the right way, thus raising the likelihood of getting impressive results.

2

———

THE STRESSFUL MIND

 Stress is a modern disease.

When our primitive ancestors met predators, their bodies secreted cortisol (a stress hormone), triggering their fight-or-flight instinct—increasing their blood sugar level, adrenaline, and reaction time to prime their body to fight or run from the predators. They might have retreated to their cave to escape the threat, and then, once safe, their cortisol hormone levels would have returned to normal.

You can't eliminate stress; you can only manage it. There is no stress-free life, no matter how hard you struggle for one. Even a peaceful monk experiences stress over possible health problems or other worries.

Some stress is useful for your mind—it keeps you motivated. Living a life with too little stress leads ultimately to boredom and low productivity.

- Military training is stressful, but it increases your toughness.
- An approaching deadline is stressful, but it motivates you to focus on your work.
- Physical exercise is stressful, but it keeps your body healthy.

Let's call this type of stress "productive stress." You need a moderate amount of this stress to keep yourself going and improving.

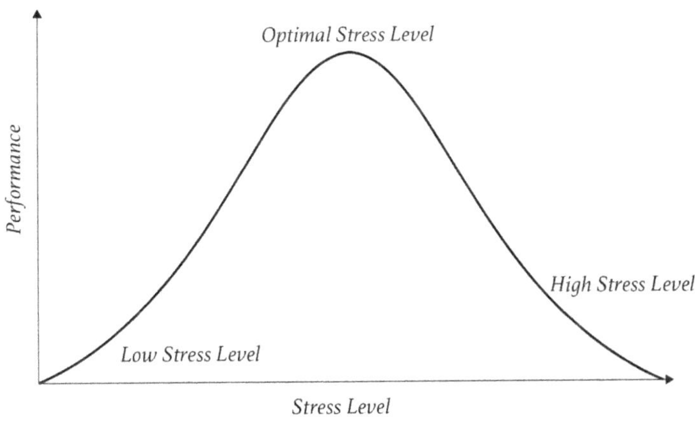

Low, Optimal, and High Stress Level Against Performance

But having too little stress is probably the least of your worries. You may already have enough—if not too much—stress to deal with.

The stress we face daily arises from:

1. An uncontrollable event

- Primitive people faced disasters, famine, predators, and bad weather.
- Modern people face economic collapse, terrorism, job loss, and irritating coworkers.

2. A controllable event

- Primitive people broke their spears, fell from slippery surfaces, and got injured while hunting.
- Modern people get woken up by jarring alarm clocks, find themselves late for meetings, and fail to turn in assignments on time.

Unlike what our primitive counterparts dealt with, the unabated stress we face often comes one incident after another. The stress from a predator encounter disappears once the threat is dealt with or escaped from, but the stress endured from backstabbing co-workers stays with you from nine to five, every day. Our ancestors might have been stressed by occasional thorns in their feet, but you may be stressed by an alarm every morning.

When you don't allow your body sufficient time to recover by exposing it to one stress after another without respite, you develop chronic stress—that is, your body continues to perceive your situation as dangerous even after the threat is over. Chronic stress leaves you with insufficient mental resources to deal with unexpected problems. As your body continues to elevate your cortisol level, it also lowers the function of your immune system, increases your chance of developing high blood pressure, and increases inflammation.[1]

There is no single anti-stress method that you can use to live a stress-free life. Relaxation techniques only provide temporary relief from stress. They don't eliminate it. Some people attempt to numb stress with alcohol, cigarettes, drugs, binge-eating, or sex, but without addressing the root cause of their stress, they will soon be bombarded with stress again after the effect wears off. No amount of relaxation can de-stress you forever from the impact of ruined relationships or chronic illnesses. Although it is possible to perform a simple relaxation technique to counter every stress encounter, such as a slow-breathing exercise, it is far more effective to eliminate as many sources of "unproductive stress" as you can.

The keys to tackling your stress levels are *minimizing* the stress that is controllable and *being resilient* through what is uncontrollable.

Minimizing Controllable Stress

HEALTH

One aspect of your life that affects your stress level in the long term is your health. Healthy sleeping habits, eating patterns, and regular exercise go a long way to strengthen your mental and physical capacity to confront stress. Dealing with major illness is particularly stressful, however.

When confronted with an ongoing stressor, we often neglect our health, forgetting that the lack thereof exacerbates our stress level further. Stress alone can also lead you to an unhealthy lifestyle:

- Stress makes you crave unhealthy food.
- Stress affects your ability to get good, quality sleep.
- Stress reduces your motivation to exercise.

If you don't make a deliberate effort to intercept this, stress will ultimately create a vicious cycle in your health. I expounded on the practical keys to optimal health in *Peak Human Clock*, so feel free to check that out if you haven't read it yet.

If you think it is worth it to lose five years of your life by smoking or living sedentarily, think again. It is not about how long you will live but about *how* you will live. Your ability to work and enjoy life will be very limited because what you really need to worry about is years—if not decades—of downward-spiralling anguish from critical illness and having to pay for expensive treatment. Unlike in past centuries, medical technology has advanced so that you can prolong your life, but your illness will eventually win out. And the ones who will suffer the most are not you but your family.

ANXIETY AND WORRY

YOU HAVE enough stress to deal with in life. Adding stress that is curated by your mind only tops up your burden. Anxiety and worry are all too common in modern life—and definitely detrimental to your stress level. This type of stress is so dreadful because when you don't overcome it, it can turn into the chronic version. It comes and goes often and exists only in your head—allowing it to attack you at any time. Whenever anxiety strikes, your stress level increases persistently—until that anxiety stops. If you are always worried, you can't give your mental resources the time they need to recover. Prolonged anxiety, if left untreated, can lead to depression and suicidal thoughts.

We have all heard these well-intentioned pieces of advice before:

- "Don't waste time worrying. Life is precious."
- "You're worrying about something that might never happen."
- "Just let it go. Mulling it over will not help you."

Sadly, this advice is not very helpful because you can't force your brain to stop worrying.

Relaxation is often prescribed as a way to treat anxiety. It helps, but we have learned that it does not solve the source of the problem. You can live with less anxiety and worry by inducing a long-term plasticity change in your brain. I elaborated in my book *Peak Brain Plasticity* on how to solve this problem from inside out rather than relying on relaxation techniques that only provide temporary cures.

OTHERS

Deal with other daily stressors in your life that are within your control. Common stressors that go unnoticed in our lives are:

- The morning rush to work
- A wake-up alarm clock
- Forgetting your car keys
- Being late for a meeting
- Failing to turn in an assignment

YOUR DAILY STRESSORS may seem minuscule and under your control, but there is no need to tax your mental resources if you can solve them. If you always have a morning rush to work, wake up earlier. If you wake up by hearing a jarring alarm clock, train your body to wake up without an alarm clock. If you always misplace your keys, set up a dedicated place to keep them. As you reduce your controllable stressors, you will save a lot of mental resources for productive activities and dealing with the inevitable twists and turns of life.

Managing Uncontrollable Stress

DO NOT ATTEMPT TO CONTROL THE UNCONTROLLABLE

A lack of control is a common culprit of stress. Trying to control the uncontrollable results in only more stress.

Imagine you have heard news that your company is preparing to restructure. You are worried that your position will be eliminated. You spend a lot of time figuring out how not to be fired. You assure yourself that you are one of the best employees there so you won't be that unlucky. The company clarifies that the restructuring has nothing to do with individual performance but with the lackluster revenue from sales—you were stressed for nothing.

If you try to control the uncontrollable, your life will be fraught with more stress. Research suggests that a stressful experience will only slightly affect you if you can find some way to perceive control.[2] Forgo controlling the uncontrollable and divert your attention to the controllable. Learning to control the controllable gives you back that sense of control and curtails your stress level. You may not always have full control over your life, but if you can just gain a little control over some aspects, you can ease your stress level.[3] You can't change your final exam schedule, but you have the control to use the remaining time to study hard and prepare for the exams.

Gaining control over the areas of your life that you can has the widespread benefit of increasing your overall stress resiliency.

It is important that you pursue hobbies you can exert high control over, such as exercising, reading, gardening, or any creative activity. You have full control over your exercise time, how many pages of a book to finish reading, what plants to grow, and how intensely you perform your sport. These give you a sense of self-worth and satisfaction. Every day, you can make and see clear progress in what you do, no matter how stressful your current situation is. This is critical to combating stress. The more stress you face in your life, the more you must work on something over which you have high control to balance your stress level.

Many elderly people lose a lot of control over their lives as they develop illnesses and disabilities. They usually experience a high level of stress when they are sent to a nursing home. A study researched two groups of elderly people in one nursing home. One group was tasked with the personal responsibility of taking care of plants, and the other was not given any responsibility. Eighteen months later, the group that was given control became healthier compared to those who were not given any control. Some of the elderly folk who were not given any task passed away.[4] It is critical for elderly individuals to remain active and feel empowered to manage their stress.

Do Not Face Stress Helplessly

HELPLESSNESS IS another cause of stress. When you are stressed, your mind amplifies the negatives of the situation, not the positives. This negativity can dominate your life and prevent you from doing something about your situation rationally. When you face your problems helplessly, all your actions will incline toward a negative bias.

- If you have an illness and feel that you are fated to never get better, your stress level increases, which deteriorates your mental health.
- If you have been fired and don't feel competent enough to get a new job, your stress level increases, which renders you ineffectual and prevents you from staying active.
- If you fail an audition and feel that you are not

talented, your stress level increases, which stops you from pursuing your dream.

Find the silver lining in every unfortunate event. Whenever you start to feel helpless, have faith that there is always a way out. This can lower your stress.[5]

- Despite any past futile attempts to cure your disease, if you continue to be active with your life, you will be less affected by stress and more likely to adopt a healthy lifestyle that may eventually help cure the disease.
- Being fired from a job does not always mean that you are not good at that job. If you have self-confidence that you will find a new one, you will be less stressed and more likely to remain productive, which increases your chance of finding a job.
- Don't beat yourself up for failing to succeed after trying hard. Acknowledge that you are a fallible human. When you make a mistake, it is part of your learning and progress, not because you are a terrible human.

People have a tendency to overestimate the impact of stress. Events that trigger major stress, such as the demise of a spouse or being a victim of a crime, are supposedly very devastating situations that many cannot fathom how to deal with. But many people are surprised to find that they are stronger than they thought. Research shows that only a small percentage of people who have experienced traumatic events end up with depression or mood disorders.[6] Everyone in the study initially experienced major grief, but most of them recovered.

The thought of stress can persist longer in your brain than the actual problems that brought about your stress, making you feel more stressed even after the problems are over. When you don't feel helpless, however, you are less affected by the actual stress.

Mindfulness Is No Stress Panacea

Mindfulness meditation is all the rage; it is taught in schools, the military, hospitals, companies, and many other establishments. Media stories tout it as the panacea that can solve nearly every problem modern humans face, from stress to poor health. Research, however, shows that the effectiveness of these claims is still in its infancy.[7] The amount of research published on mindfulness effectiveness has contributed to meditation's popularity. The acceptance of mindfulness has proliferated among the public because elite athletes, high-ranking officials, and celebrities endorse it. A Google search of "mindfulness" shows you so many alleged benefits that it may be hard to convince you otherwise.

Unfortunately, a meta-research study done showed that out of all the publications touting the benefits of mindfulness, the methodological quality of 94 percent of these publications is weak or moderately weak.[8] The remaining ones require further examination, and there were no strong conclusions as to the efficacy of its claimed benefits. A huge heap of this published research remains inconclusive because of poor-quality testing, inconsistent results, lack of rigorous standards, publication bias, or subjective self-reporting that is prone to drawing false conclusions. One study even showed that binge-drinkers scored higher in a mindfulness test than experienced meditators.[9]

The most common claim is that mindfulness obliterates anxiety and depression, but research in 2007 concluded that mindfulness does not improve either.[10] A convincing fMRI scan suggested meditators have localized brain activation in particular neuroanatomical regions. But this inference of the scanning results is flawed and overly simplistic. Performing any cognitive activity, such as playing a musical instrument or learning, also activates brain areas in neuroimaging results.[11] If the non-meditator participants breathed more rapidly during their MRI session, their results could have shown more brain activation too.[12]

There is no doubt that mindfulness has helped many people, but there are no definitive findings on the effect of mindfulness. Particular mindfulness techniques, frequencies, and durations that work for certain individuals may not work for others. Conversely, there have even been reports that mindfulness worsens depression—the very problem it is intended to solve.[13]

The practice of meditation started in Buddhism as a means for spiritual growth and understanding. Meditation practice was later reintroduced into modern society as a stress-reduction tool. The practice was secularized from dharma teachings to increase adaptability by people and unfetter it from any religious restrictions. From there, various types of avant-garde meditation practices have been conceived: transcendental meditation, Vipassana, etc. All of them use the same principles; they just offer different ways of executing them.

Note: Dharma is a religious concept that refers to the law of righteousness and truth. It is a way of living to prevent society, nature, and relationships from turning into chaos.

The calming feeling you achieve while meditating is the effect you receive when you release your body's tension at the start of the process. It has become the selling point of commercialized meditation. Achieving calmness is the goal of the practice itself. To Buddhist practitioners, releasing tension is just the beginning of the practice, the preparation to getting into a meditative state. They use meditation to foster compassion and spiritual awareness. Calmness is not the goal of their practice. It is the by-product.

Buddhist practitioners have never intended to use meditation to gain anything. Buddhist teaching prohibits clinging to anything in an attempt to avoid suffering. On the contrary, most modern practitioners use mindfulness to gain better health, greater concentration, higher-functioning brains, and other improvements. We want to gain something out of the practice, which is exactly what Buddhist practitioners want to avoid.

The surge of excitement around mindfulness as the cure for all ailments has outpaced the research. Meditation has not been proven to be superior to physical exercise or massaging in its ability to release tension if that is your primary goal. It does not yield the all-pervading, transformative power that the media claims, such as the means to your soul, mind, and body.

Here are some misleading beliefs about mindfulness:

1. Presentism is the key to happiness.

Presentism is the view that only the present exists. Your mind likes to cling to the past. Your memories keep your identity. They recall what happened before, what you ate for breakfast, why that stranger stared at you, or why you said those remarks to your friend. All these events make up who and how you are now.

Your mind also likes to imagine future events because it longs to control the future. It thinks of what to do next when you are still doing something else. You feel slow and helpless if you don't let your mind think about the future. After all, your wandering mind has likely saved you from forgetting to do something or missing out on something on multiple occasions.

Your mind feels safe when oscillating between past and future events. It feels scary to let go of your mental chatter completely. What else will be your royal assistant and persistently remind you of your shortcomings (past) so that you can improve and of what to do next (future) so that you don't miss out on anything?

Mainstream mindfulness practitioners claim that this mental chatter brings suffering to your life and that the only way to attain ultimate happiness and a stress-free life is to live in the now permanently. You can't feel both positive and negative experiences at the same time. You can't feel contentment (positive) and resentment (negative) at the same time. You can't feel regretful (past) when you are in the present. You can't feel hopeful (future) when you are in the present. The present is just what it is. You see no problems at all unless you are currently faced with an immediate threat.

From moment to moment, this can feel calming, but to live in the present permanently in your quest for happiness is fallacious. Disregarding the past and future permanently is merely a means of escaping reality. Reality requires that you consider tomorrow (and decades later) so you will still have food to eat, money to spare for your children's education, or a healthy body to count on. Reality requires that you look back at the past to learn from mistakes and make decisions. Life is shallow without the past and purposeless without the future.

During the course of our early evolution, our ancestors lived completely in the present. They ate whenever they were hungry and procreated whenever they wanted to. There was no concern of yesterday or tomorrow. They had only the present to savor. They lived similarly to how apes live today. As humans evolved into *Homo neanderthalensis*, nature gifted us with the frontal lobe.[14] This is the part of the brain that handles reasoning and thinking and grants you the ability to remember the past and plan for the future. It gives birth to mental chatter.

Now, it is not possible for you to stay in the present forever because you have a frontal lobe. You need this part of your brain to function in the modern world:

- To know when to avoid unhealthy food
- To know not to mate with another's spouse
- To save money for tomorrow

Staying fully in the present would eradicate these past and future-based thoughts. Imagine how abnormal it would be to live completely in the present while ignoring the past and future. A time without tomorrow. We would live like animals. If it's at all possible, to live fully in the present is to also let go of your mental sense of auto-pilot that helps you form habits. Staying mindfully in the present all the time would exhaust your mental resources. Buddhist meditation practice does not support presentism either.[15]

2. Be non-judgmental.

Many advocates of mindfulness encourage you to meditate when you are stressful. The problem you are experiencing is said to originate from your mind, not anything external. All the world's problems live in your head. To solve your problem is to control your mind and accept the world as it is with no judgment; so, if you are stressed, it is your mental problem and not others'. If everyone in the world meditates, the world will be a better place. This perception attempts to absolve all problems.

Meditation mollifies your mind briefly as you retreat into your private mental sphere, but any actual problems remain unresolved. You will still return to reality after meditating. There is no way you can be free of your problems if you surrender your life to the circumstances around you. Your problems will still persist if you abandon any effort to solve them.

DON'T OBSESS over mastering mindfulness to reach happiness or free yourself from misery because the technique will never be able to give you those benefits. If mindfulness is treated as the holy grail for all worldly problems, one's behavior can be conditioned to disengage from society and retreat into one's private sphere, making that individual reluctant to solve problems. This behavior also intensifies one's attachment to the practice itself. Practicing mindfulness meditation will not make you stress-free.

Certainly, modern meditation has its own merits if you are not seeking to reach enlightenment, treat a disorder, or disregard your problems. You can use it to:

1. Regain focus.

When you are overwhelmed with work and the weight of many tasks, your mind tends to lose focus in the face of so many distractions. Mindfulness meditation keeps your focus on a single object, such as your breathing or a candle flame. It trains your brain to filter out cloudy thoughts and regain focus so that you can make space for clearer thinking.

2. Gain emotional and impulse control.

Mindfulness meditation trains you to detect your wandering mind. You can become astute at noticing automatic reactions influenced by your impulses and emotions, and you can then will yourself to be mindful whenever you need to—not switching it on permanently, however, lest you waste a lot of mental resources. Every time you are angry, sad, or fearful, pause to watch how your mind attempts to control your physical reactions. Watch how uncomfortable the feelings of anger, sadness, or fear are.

Make no mistake, these are feelings that make you human. There is no reason to deny them. Your only goal is to not let these emotions control you or turn you violent. Do not judge your thoughts because you will only feed them and let them grow stronger. When anger comes in, trying to suppress it because you label it as a bad emotion only makes it rebound stronger.[16] The part of your brain called the amygdala detects your message that there is a threat, and it begins to trigger your fight-or-flight response, increasing your heart rate, elevating your adrenaline, and causing your blood pressure to surge to prepare you for a fight.

When you accept the uncomfortable feeling of anger without letting it control you, the anger will gradually reduce, and you will develop a tendency to stay calm and in control.

SINCE STRESS IS an inescapable part of your life, it is pivotal that you learn to manage it well. When you overcome a new level of stress, you become much better at coping with your stress the next time. Researchers at the University of California found that people who had previously been exposed to high stress and survived grew stronger and reported less stress in any recent unpleasant experiences they had dealt with.[17]

Don't view inevitable stressors as your enemy but as the source of your progress. And by giving yourself a sufficient recovery period, you are building yourself into a better person through how you deal with stress.

Stressful experiences are never pleasant, but focusing your energy on negativity only makes your stress worse and hampers your progress.[18] Research shows that positive emotions relieve stress physically and mentally. When a group of participants subjected to intense cardiovascular activity was asked to view a film that elicited contentment, they recovered faster than another group that viewed a film that elicited sadness or neutrality.[19] This study highlights how you can lower your stress level with positive emotions.

Now we have covered the topic of stress. We will next look at the subject of happiness and how to minimize unhappiness to keep your mind healthy.

3

THE HAPPINESS DECEPTION

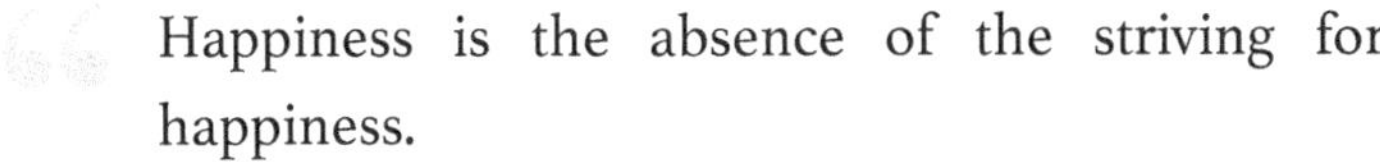

Happiness is the absence of the striving for happiness.

— ZHUANG ZHOU

EVERYONE IN THE WORLD WORKS HARD FOR HAPPINESS AND DOES everything in their power to attain it. Many psychologists, scientists, and experts conveniently ascribe 90 percent of your happiness to what's inside your mind, not external factors. They've used success stories of those who claim to be happy, coupled with some scientific studies, to package advice aimed at working on your mind in order to reach happiness.

Positive psychology has inexorably taken the world by storm, influencing people to internalize all their problems into their own lives. The general message is that if you are unhappy, it is your problem. It is your lack of strength in handling your mind. All unhappiness is reduced to being the by-product of problems in your mind. When you are unhappy, you are told to fix your mind by meditating or thinking positively and that happiness cannot happen by itself and must be earned. Sadly, this is a *prima facie* belief, and the concept has created a tumultuous reality.

Happiness has been commercialized into a multibillion-dollar industry. Apps have been developed to measure your level of happiness using games that have no way of knowing what makes you happy. These companies often use the profundities of medical experts to back their claims in promulgating their happiness products, courses, or books.

Happiness apps perturb and make you feel dissatisfied with yourself. An app that claims to gauge your happiness level more than you can makes you rely on the program to decide if you are happy or not. Your happiness level is quantified by the app. You need to constantly monitor the app to keep your happiness level in check. You are never perfectly happy and always need correction. Even if you have no mental problems, you will always feel bereft. Daily use of the app implants disconcerting thoughts into your subconsciousness. Remember that when your subconsciousness wants to believe something as true, it will see it as if it is the truth.

The most convenient solution for any problem that creates unhappiness seems to be telling people to look inward and fix their mindset. They can be happy if they want to. We are made to believe that we are imperfect until we attain the self-betterment needed to reach happiness. We are offered advice on how to tame our mind to be happy and how we can still be happy in the face of mistreatment, injustice, poor living conditions, and other plights. These concepts of happiness are useful in producing obedient citizens, workers, and military members. Meanwhile, any misconduct or wrong-doing done by a corporation that makes employees unhappy is brushed off and remains uncorrected. It has become the responsibility of employees to make themselves happy, not that of their employers. If corporate culture is bad and employees are unhappy, it is the employees' problem. Employers want happy employees but don't want to do what it takes to make them happy. Any actual solutions that could make employees happy are kept to a minimum to save cost, time, or effort. There is no need for better public service, a better education system, better healthcare, or a safer environment if happiness can be reached within one's mind.

This mindset is inimical and promotes individualism and self-centeredness. As a result, people become uppity. Everyone directs attention to themselves—instead of others—because that is the only way they feel they can lift their happiness. As people are made to feel accountable for being unhappy, their sense of helplessness increases. They feel bad and guilty about themselves when they are unhappy. Because of this insecurity and its potential threat to self-esteem, people put on a façade of happiness while concealing how they really feel. They tend to give higher-than-average ratings when asked in questionnaires if they are happy, which belies the survey results. People also want to appear as happy as possible in their social media posts to emulate others' awesome lives. The fact is, they are unlikely to be as happy as they appear. Unhappiness is perceived as a sign of defeat and failure and often greeted with derision or rejection.

Despite the burgeoning positive psychology advice on happiness and the claim that we are happier than ever before in human history, the suicide rate continues to climb, and millions of people seek therapy for their unhappiness every year.

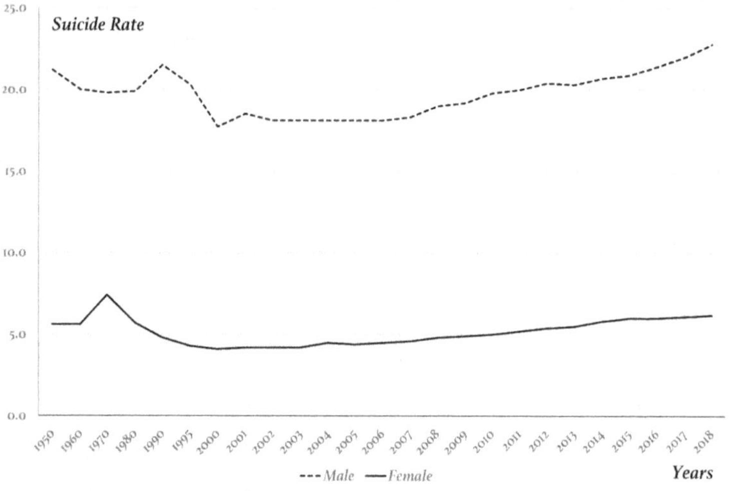

Suicides per 100,000 Residents in the US

You can't completely control your own happiness. Your circumstances play a part in determining your level of happiness. If there is a problem in your workplace, you can't possibly enjoy your work entirely and be happy. Problems that make you unhappy must still be resolved. In-sourcing happiness in your mind whenever you are unhappy is exhausting and does not solve the real problems.

There Is No Bad Emotion

Positive psychologists bedevil "bad" emotions—anger, envy, guilt, hatred, sadness—and want you to stay away from these emotions in order to be happy.

- The racial injustice movement in the 1960s would never have succeeded if everyone were just faking happiness so as to accept being unfairly treated.
- Countries such as the US would never have gained independence if no one had been around to express hatred and resentment toward colonial power.
- Companies might never feel the need to improve if there are no vociferous customers who show dissatisfaction.

None of these could succeed and make the world a better place if everyone stayed clear of negative emotions. Jealousy could fuel your motivation to try harder. Fear could make you take more precautionary measures.

These emotions make you human, and there is no reason to remove them in the name of gaining happiness. Living without these negative emotions discolors your life.

- There would be no mourning upon the demise of a family member.
- There would be no guilt after cheating on one's spouse.
- There would be no fear following excitement during

sky-diving—fear that ensures you pull your parachute in time.

In short, all emotions are good for your well-being. There is no need to avoid negative emotions or obsess over positive emotions. Stop blaming yourself for being sad, angry, or unhappy.

There Is No Constant State of Happiness

We expect that happiness is reaped upon the fulfillment of certain goals, such as getting that raise or buying that dream house. These are what motivate us to work hard. Happiness is the end in itself. The truth is, after getting what you are after, the happiness you earned wears off. You go back to your neutral state, and your tolerance to feeling happiness increases. You can become trapped in a vicious cycle of coveting more just to remain happy. Psychologists call this phenomenon hedonic adaptation. This is the tendency for one's happiness level to return to its base level relatively soon after positive or negative change. We crave that happiness again, and our desire for more increases once we fulfil one goal. This makes achieving permanent happiness impossible, no matter how much you gain in life.

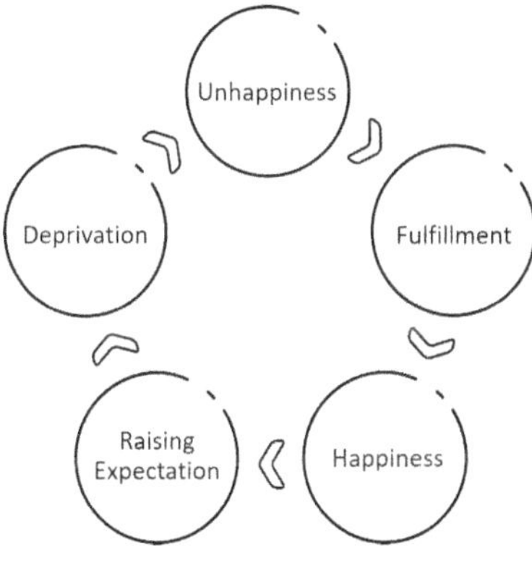

Hedonic Adaptation

Your base level of happiness is subjective and relative to your present state. A beggar could be exhilarated when he receives a package of food, while a rich man could just feel neutral when he receives the same. When what you are deprived of is fulfilled, you are happy. A beggar could be deprived of a pair of shoes, while a rich man could be deprived of a swanky Ferrari.

No one lives in a permanent state of happiness. Your happiness level goes up and down. For every desire that is fulfilled, your happiness rises and then returns to its base level shortly afterward. Similarly, when you encounter an unhappy moment, your happiness lowers and then returns to its base level shortly afterward.

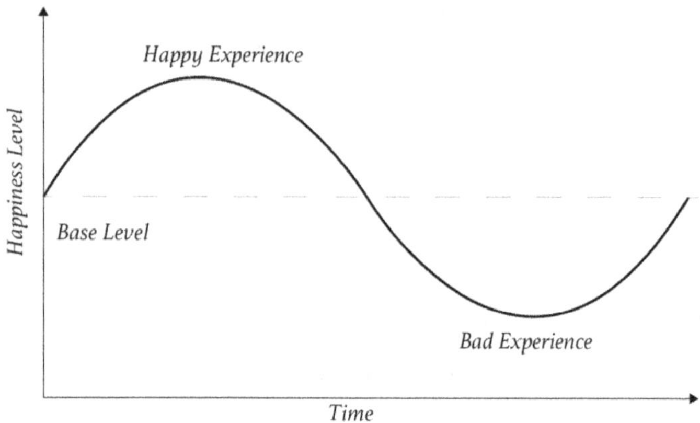

The Rise and Fall of Happiness from Positive and Negative Experiences

Jackpot winners experience felicity initially but soon adjust to their new wealth, and their happiness level returns to its base level again. Accident victims who lose their limbs are devastated at the beginning, but they soon adapt to the situation, and their happiness level returns to the same level it was at before the accident.[1] Moreover, because of their new state, these people could end up happier than they were before because they can now derive enjoyment from gestures formerly seen as insignificant: chatting with friends, eating with family members, and receiving care from caregivers.

The onset of inconceivable distress, such as losing a child or your limbs, can turn your life upside down initially but also has a chance to make you happier afterward as your mind adapts to savor positivity in your life and begins to treasure more of what you are left with. Your subconsciousness has a mechanism to locate positivity when experiencing extremely unpleasant events. The situation is called cognitive dissonance. Even if there is no positivity in your problem, your mind will somehow distort the truth to make up a positive takeaway and alter your attitude to ameliorate the devastation and help your mental health cope.[2]

Ironically, this does not work when the unpleasant feeling is not horrendous enough.[3] Your mind does not automatically dig positivity out of a moderately unpleasant experience. That's why some people are willing to stick around in a struggling relationship (intensely unpleasant) but unwilling to forgive their spouse who leaves dirty socks on the bedroom floor (moderately unpleasant).

In addition, the problem with this mental mechanism is that you don't begin to feel grateful until you experience undeserved suffering. After learning how your mind works, I hope you can intentionally take advantage of life's pleasures right now without waiting for your mind to do it when you suffer intensely.

The Paradox of Happiness

Pursuing happiness is a never-ending quest. If you think you will be happy only after getting or achieving something, then you will never be truly happy.

Having the motivation to pursue happiness is beneficial to keep you working toward new goals, and there is nothing wrong with that. The only drawback is that you only receive short-term happiness when your goal is fulfilled, while you may have spent years of your life slaving away at something unhappily to reach the goal.

All of us, one way or another, need to go through unhappy moments to create a better state of life as a whole. Some need to endure unhappiness longer, while others are lucky to only suffer for a short while.

- You need to go through years of education, no matter how much you despise school.
- You might need to go through years of military service, even if you don't care about it.
- You might need to go through years of tending an infant into adulthood, despite how tiresome it is.

You are fortunate if you enjoy school life, serving in the military, or taking care of babies, but not everyone is the same. Positive psychologists generalize all problems as being due to individuals who cannot enjoy their work. It is easy to condemn these individuals, but you just can't force any human trait, including enjoying a particular task. Besides, there is nothing wrong with disliking what you dislike.

Those who are happy doing what they do end up doing that activity better because happiness fuels motivation and performance.[4] When you are happy in the progress toward your goal, you are more likely to succeed.

- Musicians who enjoy making songs make better songs.
- Painters who enjoy creating art paint better.
- Authors who write books they enjoy working on are usually more successful than ones who simply want to finish their books.

Intuitively, these happy people have better well-being and fare better than their unhappy counterparts.[5] Their happiness toward the work they are doing enables better creativity (better work), higher physical immunity (less downtime), and an increased output of work (higher productivity).

The takeaway is to consider your skills and interest in the subject when making a long-term decision if you have a choice. Studying for a PhD to earn a high social rank so that you will be happy is an enormous waste of time. After you complete the five years of study, which you would hate, you would finally earn your reward: People could now call you "Doctor." But you still wouldn't feel fulfilled. When you make happiness the end goal in your mind, without being happy with the process, you will waste many years of effort just to get that piece of transitory happiness.

If you study for a PhD because you want to conduct research and are inquisitive about a topic that you enjoy, you have a higher chance of succeeding satisfactorily. You would be happy to attend lectures. You would put extra effort into completing the study because you'd enjoy the process. You would not be just seeking to earn a title to be happy.

Don't expect happiness at the completion of your goal, but work on things that can keep you happy while you persist through to your goal.

The Happy Hormone

Scientists have suggested that a "happiness trait" may be inherited at birth.[6] Even if this is true, your environment and lifestyle still affect your happiness, no matter how good your genes are. Instead of focusing on genes that you can't change, let's look at the combination of biological hormones that can induce the feeling of happiness.

The four neurotransmitters in your body that are responsible for making you happy are dopamine, serotonin, oxytocin, and endorphin.

- Dopamine is released when you experience pleasure, anticipate pleasure, complete your tasks, and reach your goals.
- Serotonin regulates your mood. Depression and stress lower serotonin.
- Oxytocin is a love hormone that is produced when you cuddle, bond, or make love.
- Endorphins promote relaxation and induce happiness through pain reduction.

To feel happy naturally, you must increase the levels of these neurotransmitters.

Dopamine

People can exploit the release of this hormone through playing video games, watching pornography, and eating junk food. You will get a jolt of happiness when you do one of these activities, but it will be at a cost to your well-being and health. The alternatives to these are:

1. Have something to look forward to.

Do you recall a moment in your childhood when you couldn't wait for your Christmas vacation? Recall how happy you were just by anticipating the moment. Receiving a reward releases dopamine, but research confirms that anticipating a reward releases dopamine too.[7]

Dr. Robert Sapolsky conducted an experiment to measure a monkey's dopamine level when anticipating a reward versus when receiving the reward. He trained the monkey to press a button ten times when a light appeared. Food would be dispensed at the tenth button press. Here's the interesting thing: The monkey's dopamine level was elevated during the anticipation and plummeted after receiving the reward. The dopamine release was elevated even higher if the outcome was only 50 percent certain.

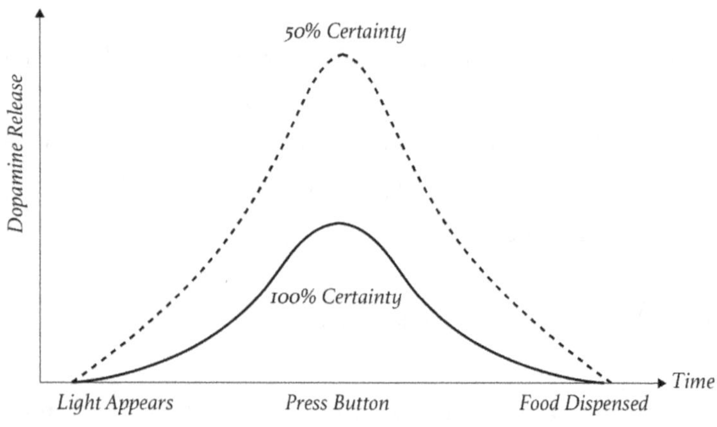

Dopamine Release on a Certain vs Uncertain Outcome

Anticipating a reward is more pleasurable than getting one. Purposely delaying rewards can keep the pleasure coming. Movie directors often inject teasers at the end of their movies to maintain strong anticipation before the release of the next movie. Gambling is so addictive because the anticipation of winning the jackpot and the uncertainty of winning create a surge in one's dopamine release.

If you set up a few pleasurable future plans that you are anticipating few months or a year in advance, you can deliberately renew your interest every day by reminding yourself of what you have planned. A future plan could be:

- A family vacation
- Eating your favorite food
- A weekend outing

Just as anticipating a future reward is more pleasurable than the reward itself, anticipating future punishment is more unpleasant than the punishment itself. Psychologists conducted an experiment with two groups of volunteers.[8] One group was set to receive twenty high-intensity shocks but was given a warning three seconds before receiving a shock. The other group was set to receive three high-intensity shocks and seventeen low-intensity shocks with no warnings. Being unable to predict their punishment, the group receiving three random high-intensity shocks had their hearts beat faster and rated themselves as more afraid than the group receiving twenty predictable high-intensity shocks.

Despite the wariness of waiting for a punishment, you might still cling to that feeling because you want to feel as if you are on top of the situation to reduce the impact it will cause.

Having a long-haul project can be draining but satisfying at the same time if you anticipate the successful completion of your project. If you always have something to look forward to, you can wake up every morning feeling enthusiastic about conquering your day.

2. Have a meaningful life goal.

When you successfully complete a difficult task, you can challenge yourself with an even more difficult one. You will get better every day and feel confident enough to take on any difficult challenge.

If you have a choice, it is crucial that you pursue goals that give meaning to your life, even if that means forgoing a high salary because when your activities are meaningful to you, you have the extra fuel to stick with them.[9]

A teacher who perceives his/her work as a calling to educate the next generation gains more happiness in return when compared to those who view the job as a career. A pediatrician who loves dealing with children would go the extra mile in prescribing treatment to children. The work becomes personal and rewarding in itself. Certainly, not everyone has the luxury to choose the job best suited for them, but you can pursue hobbies that give meaning to your life.

3. Reach your highest potential.

Being able to reach your full potential is a deeply satisfying feeling. If you have a chance to exert a signature skill every day, you can be significantly happier than when you don't use your skills at all.[10] When you use a skill every day, you continuously get better at it. If swimming is your forte, you would be much happier spending time training to get into an Olympic competition than working at a high-paying, desk-bound job.

The adage "follow your passion" is destructive to your mindset. If you must discover your passion first before you work on something, you will never do anything. You will have turned away a lot of rewarding opportunities on the basis that they are not your passion. Passion is never gifted to you at birth. Instead, you develop passion as you start working and enjoying your work.

A successful farmer is not born with the passion to raise crops; a famous singer is not born with the passion to sing; a superstar teacher is not born with the passion to teach. They develop their passions for planting, singing, and teaching as they do the work. Passion does not discover these people; these people discover their passions.

Not only are you not born with your predetermined passion, but you can also develop new passions as you go. A passionate bodybuilder can also be passionate about acting and running for a government office; a passionate scientist can be passionate about writing science-fiction books. The only thing required of you to discover your passions is to start.

If you have anything you have been meaning to do and have the resources to support it, please go for it without waiting for your passion to appear.

SEROTONIN

I ELABORATED on the methods to gain sufficient serotonin in another book, *Peak Self-Control*. The gist of them are:

- Maintain a low stress level daily to avoid the reduction of serotonin.
- Eliminate coffee and alcohol, which reduce serotonin.
- Maintain a healthy lifestyle. Exercise and sleep enough.
- Get enough sunlight.
- Consume food containing tryptophan.

Oxytocin

Methods of increasing your levels of oxytocin include the following:

1. Gain social support.

Study after study have concluded that people with strong social support are the happiest.[11] This type of study has been successfully replicated repeatedly. The correlation between one's social support level and their happiness level is higher than the correlation between tobacco and cancer. Paradoxically, our family members—the ones with the strongest social connection to us and who will stand by us in hard times—are usually the first we neglect in our tireless pursuit of happiness. When was the last time you ignored your kid while you were checking your Instagram? Did you snap at your spouse when you were overly stressed by your work? We destroy the very source of our happiness in the process of achieving our goals, which we falsely believe will lead to infinite happiness.

Many people willingly sacrifice their source of happiness for success because they believe they can earn happiness again after succeeding and buy back their lost happiness afterward. When they succeed at their goal, they look back at the years they spent chasing dollars and realize that their success cannot buy back the time they wish they could have spent with their parents or children because their aging parents have passed away or their children have grown up to be strangers.

Cancer patients have a lower risk of death when they have strong ties with their social contacts.[12] When you have trusted family members, neighbors, colleagues, and friends to count on, you lessen the impact of any difficulty that you may face in your life. You feel that you don't have to carry all your heavy burdens alone.

- Strong social support lowers the risk of depression.[13]
- Strong social support may lower the risk of cardiovascular disease.[14]
- Strong social support increases the ability to recover from stress and reduces the perception of stressful situations as stressful.[15]

Having trusted relationships with others make people happy because of the release of oxytocin. As a social being, you want to avoid being lonely as much as possible. It not only is harmful to your well-being but also deteriorates your brain cells. It is worth a life spent cultivating good connections with people to live happier and healthier.

Happiness is spreadable. People have the tendency to mimic the behavior of those they spend the most time with. If you want to be happy, surround yourself with happy people. Being the closest to you, your family members bear the biggest influence. If your spouse always comes home angry, you won't be eager to share any good news with him/her. Your child will be reticent with your spouse. You may end up having a lot of fights with your spouse due to lack of communication and trust. Your child learns to be grumpy and brings that unhappiness to school too.

Now, imagine your spouse is a happy person. Your kid is eager to see him/her come home. You are keen to discuss anything with him/her. Everyone is happy doing things together. You see how easy one family member's unhappiness spreads to the entire family and then to each member of their social network.

Your brain consists of mirror neurons that are fired when you act out or observe the same action done by others. For example:

- You watch a scene of an actor falling, and your body moves as if it is falling too.
- When someone smiles at you, you smile back at him/her unconsciously.
- You yawn when you see someone else yawning.

This mirroring mechanism lets you empathize with others by interpreting their facial expressions. That's why comedy shows use canned laughter to trigger the same effect in us. A study shows that viewers are likely to laugh or perceive a joke as funny when it is followed by canned laugher.[16]

Because mirror neurons make you prone to stimulate others' behavior, the people you spend the most time with play a major role in influencing your happiness. You don't have control over the moods of people surrounding you, but you can at least be the one to spread joy to your social circle.

2. Perform acts of kindness.

Being kind to others releases oxytocin.[17] Make a conscious goal to perform at least one kind act every day to be happier.

- Help an elderly person carry heavy grocery bags.

- Hold an elevator for strangers.
- Pick up litter.
- Buy food for a beggar.

ENDORPHINS

Endorphins act similar to drugs for relieving pain. Endorphins are released when you are hurt to keep you going and stimulate feelings of happiness. Endorphins can also be released through the following activities:

1. Laughter

The easiest and least invasive way to get an endorphin release is to laugh.[18] Research shows that pain tolerance increases by 10 percent after laughing.[19] Because of the painkiller effect of laughter, some hospitals administer laughing gas as an option for labor pain relief.

2. Exercise

Another way to elevate your endorphin level is to exercise. Long-distance runners sometimes experience euphoria while running, called a runner's high. This is endorphins in action.

Various types of exercise release endorphins differently:

- Both aerobic and anaerobic exercises increase endorphins at the same rate.[20]

- Low-intensity exercise releases few endorphins.[21]
- High-intensity exercise releases lots of endorphins.[22]
- When low-intensity exercise turns high-intensity, causing your muscles to build up a lot of lactic acid, a significant amount of endorphins are released.[23] This happens when low-intensity aerobic exercise lasts for more than an hour or when anaerobic exercise is done in many repetitions.

Learning the various ways you can use exercise to trigger endorphins can help you stick to the habit of exercising. Incorporate some intense exercises in your routine to keep you motivated for longer and happier.

3. Food

The University of Turku showed in a 2017 study that satisfying your satiety releases endorphins, but eating highly palatable food, such as pizza, ice cream, or chocolate releases even more endorphins.[24] Because of the enormous endorphin release, it is easy to overeat and get addicted to junk food, leading to obesity. When you are in a foul mood, you subconsciously want to reach for this comfort food to get a surge of endorphins.

The good thing is that you can use spicy food as an alternative. Spicy food activates the pain receptors in your tongue and tricks your brain into releasing endorphins.[25] It pays for your long-term health to train your tongue to eat spicy food instead of junk food.

4. Music

Music evokes emotion and induces relaxation. Research confirms that listening to music releases endorphins that also help with pain relief.[26] A study in 1998 showed that students listening to techno music increased their level of endorphins significantly.[27] As this research only used one type of music, it remains unclear if there are other types that can stimulate different levels of endorphin production. A larger sample size and wide variety of music types are needed to quantify this finding further. Thus, you'd better listen to the songs that you enjoy.

When you are sad, however, listening to an uplifting song can aggravate your sadness. It makes you feel that the whole world is happy while you are sad. On the other hand, listening to sad music makes you feel better because your mirror neurons make you feel that you are not the only one who is sad.[28] This feeling helps you cope with your sadness.[29]

5. Touch

All kinds of touch, including professional massages, hand-holding, making love, and friendly touches, release endorphins and oxytocin to increase bonding and reduce tension and pain. All the little hugs you give to your children help them grow happier and healthier.

NOT EVERY DAY is roses and flowers. You will experience unhappy moments in life, but you can lighten the effect of them by doing activities that contribute to your happiness. The psychological effects of a single unhappy experience outweigh those of a single happy experience. Some studies indicate that it takes three positive experiences to ward off one negative experience.[30] Some say it takes five positive experiences. It is hard to quantify the count since happiness is a subjective feeling. Whatever the number may be, the more happiness you can experience, the more immune you are to the effect of unhappiness.

Perception of Money

A discussion of happiness would be incomplete without talking about money. Money is the top goal for many people seeking to be happy. A common adage is "Money cannot buy happiness." It is true that money cannot buy every type of happiness, but it does buy some. Actually, a *lot* of happiness. You can make others happy by giving, and the best thing that money can buy is the freedom of using your time however you like. That is, the ability to do anything you want, whenever you want, and however you want without worrying if you will still have food to eat tomorrow or enough funds to deal with an emergency. Remember that a lack of control is the root of stress. When you have enough money to control your own schedule, you release a lot of stress and are happier.

Modern society requires that you have sufficient money to buy happiness. How much is enough? A famous study by Princeton University shows that once you have an annual income of

$75,000 per year, any additional money in your bank account does not make you happier.[31] The study suggests that money does very little to increase your happiness after it lifts you out of poverty and into the middle class. A later study by Purdue University concluded that a $95,000 yearly income is needed to be happy.[32]

Don't rely on these figures. Happiness is subjective. You may be living in an area with a higher cost of living or education, or you may have a fulfilling hobby that is pricey. You may be a middle-class citizen, but without having unreserved assurance that you will have more than enough to pay for your bills, your home mortgage loan, your children's ever-increasing education fees, or unforeseen hospitalization needs, you will always be in a precarious financial situation. Note that these are just the basic necessities of modern humans. We have not yet considered other expensive purchases that might be needed to create a fulfilling life such as buying a cello to play, paying a course fee to expand your studies, or buying a decent camera to learn photography. All of these need money. Low life satisfaction and fulfillment do not make you truly happy.

SOME SURMISE MONEY TO be the cause of many problems. Money is just a tool, and when used properly, is a road to happiness. When it causes problems, it is always problems with one's attitude toward money. If you know how to use your money, you can buy almost everything that is not directly purchasable by money.

- Money cannot buy relationships, trust, and respect, but you can use money to buy books and learn how to be a better person.
- Money cannot buy good health, but you can use your money to hire a professional health coach and buy a gym membership.
- And much more.

Here are some common pitfalls in some people's relationship with money in the search for happiness that can end up making them more unhappy:

Irrational Spending

Despite the fact that the probability of winning the lottery is one in a few million, many people continue to buy lottery tickets instead of investing their money. The *Journal of Gambling Studies* conducted a review in 2011 and found that the majority of lottery ticket buyers are poor people who cannot afford to fork out the same amount for emergency needs.[33] Since it gives them the ability to control the numbers they pick, the lottery makes people feel that they can win.[34] Psychologists call it the illusion of control—that is, the tendency for people to overestimate their ability to control an outcome.

A person's relationship with money depends profoundly on their upbringing and past experiences. People who have lived through poverty make different investment decisions than people who are born rich, and there is no right or wrong way of handling money. To you, the lottery is a bet that you may not win in your lifetime, while to others, it is their only chance to escape from poverty, given that the lottery offers the same chance of winning for everyone, rich or poor. If betting on the lottery gives you a tiny hope for your future, then go on, but if you want a good night's sleep, the rule of thumb is not to risk an amount that you can't afford to lose.

GREED

CERTAINLY, an obsession over money causes greed and makes you forsake much more important things just to earn more money when you already have more than enough. This mindset brings forth a compulsion to engage in risky trading, irresponsible borrowing, or even fraud.

Mr. K was a millionaire. By any definition, he was rich enough to do anything he wanted in his entire life. But it didn't end there. He had the ambition to earn the title "billionaire." In his search for a quicker way to reach that goal, he took part in an insider trading scheme that landed him in prison. He sacrificed every piece of his happiness and freedom for what he did not need.

An insatiable appetite for more money can cause you to lose sight of what's more important in your life: your family, identity, reputation, and freedom. There is no need to risk what you need for what you don't.

SOCIAL COMPARISON

PEOPLE HAVE the tendency to want to be at least on par with their peers. Those who have a critical illness are apt to compare themselves to others who are in worse conditions to feel better. Bronze winners compare themselves downward to those who completed the competition with no medal and therefore are happier than silver winners, who compare themselves to gold winners.[35]

The same goes for money. Say you earn $500,000 a year and can comfortably cover all your family's needs. Your cousin lives in a larger house, and you don't feel satisfied until you buy one yourself. So, you decide to live in a more affluent society by getting a loan and relocating to an aristocratic maisonette with a sea view in the Bahamas. You later spot your neighbor with a Porsche car. You feel compelled to get one even though you have never been a fan of racing cars. You take out another loan and buy that car so that you can face your new neighbor with pride. You are not any happier now after upgrading your lifestyle and getting that car, for you have accumulated a large debt to pay off. That $500,000 annual salary may seem like a lot of money to many people who need to work multiple jobs just to get by and could make them really happy, but it has led you to unhappiness.

Financial stress from debt is very real. Many people spend their lives working at jobs they hate to pay off their creditors. No matter how much you make, attempting to compare your wealth with others is futile because there is always someone richer than you or who owns better items than you do. When you always compare your wealth to that of others, you will inflate your lifestyle beyond your means and reduce your savings.

Illusion of Richness

HUMANS ARE OFTEN myopic toward the future. A one-time success can give you an illusion that you will be continuously wealthy. You begin to underestimate the risks that could bring you down. Many celebrities have fallen victim to this illusion and splurged their wealth away.

A successful investor could be wrong most of the time but still make a lot of money by being correct a few times. But the same odds could make other investors go bankrupt. No matter how successful you are now, you can't assume that you will stay that way tomorrow. Save and invest some money, for tomorrow may be a rainy day.

Choosing a Job for Its Earning Power

IF YOU WANT happiness and have the luxury to choose a job, never choose one because of its earning power. A simple way to check if you are truly happy with your job is to ask yourself if you always wake up in the morning feeling energized to work. If you do, you have found your dream job and workplace.

The biggest precursor of happiness at work is not your paycheck but your autonomy.[36] This is the ability to make decisions and be flexible with your time as long as you can complete the work on time. Jobs with low autonomy circumscribe your lunchtime and require you to systematically complete task after task at a pace that you have very little control over. Always strive to prioritize choosing a job with high autonomy.

Certainly, jobs with good autonomy are not easy to come by. The advancement of technology also lowers the autonomy of workers. A few decades ago, when you left work, you had freedom over your time until the next day when you went to the office again. Now, with technology that enables instant communication through smartphones, your freedom of time is reduced significantly because your boss can contact you at any time of the day. Society is now, on average, richer but not happier than it was generations ago.

If you have a job with good autonomy, try your best to hang onto it. If you don't have one, it is worth taking a shot at a career switch if your situation permits because, if you spend the next thirty years in the same job, you'll want to be happy doing it.

You may stay at a job you dislike for a long time because it suits the field you chose during college many years ago. But humans are bad at predicting their future happiness. What you thought would be your ideal career ten years ago may not seem so ideal today. What you thought would be your ideal country to live in may not hold true now. No one—not even you—knows what will make your future self happy. You may realize now that the choice of field you made at college is not what you really want. As you grow older and discover the type of work that you really like, don't be afraid to make a career switch. The longer you wait, the more difficult this will become as you get older and have less opportunity to learn. If you must stay at your job to fulfil your financial obligations, make the most out of the job while you prepare yourself for a future career switch such as taking relevant courses after work or pursuing related education. Life is too short to continue working unhappily.

Many people would rather toil away at a job they dislike to earn a high paycheck even if they have a choice to switch to a job they like. People usually find the material reward too attractive to leave the job. Humans spend about ninety thousand hours working in their lifetime. Spending this tremendous amount of time at a job that you dislike is a waste of your time and happiness.

If you are not struggling to make ends meet, keep your spending conservative and strike a balance between your paycheck and your happiness. You don't want to have to get by on a meager income, lest you are unprepared for your retirement. You also don't want to slave away almost all your time in a cubicle to earn top dollar, lest you regret having no time for your younger self and your children.

Material Purchases

If you think owning posh items makes you look rich or classy, think again. What most people actually do is imagine themselves looking rich owning what you own, not admiring you as a smart and wealthy person. At worst, this only invites envy.

This mindset is rooted in many people who go out of their way to show off and convince others of their economic success because furnishing their outward appearance is easier than showing their bank account balance to others. Certainly, this is not meant to discourage you from buying fancy stuff. You can if you like. Just note that if admiration is what you are looking for, fancy stuff does not do anything besides deplete your savings and investment opportunities.

Buy materials that you need to use, not to earn admiration. Purchases that cannot be seen by others often make you happier than material purchases that can be seen by others. You are what you achieve, not what you buy.

THE WORLD MUST KEEP DANGLING carrots in front of people so that they can continue the rat race and keep the economy running. It needs people to continuously spend money and to believe that consuming goods makes them happy. You are presented with tantalizing advertisements to purchase goods with the promise of happiness. If everyone stops buying, the economy will collapse.

Family Disharmony

Your direct family members play a big role in your happiness because you spend the most time with them. When you are planning to start a family, adopting the right mindset can make a world of difference in your life.

Marriage

A STUDY in 2016 found that happiness in married life is affected by how similar partners are to each other.[37] During your youth, you probably considered attractiveness as the primary factor when selecting your life partner. Most people do (including myself). If you want lasting happiness in marriage, though, you should choose a partner close to you in age who has a similar mindset to yours: similar habits, same views on religion, same ways of living, same pursuits, same values, and economic background, as well. These will go a long way in keeping your married life happy. Even in a disagreement, both of you will be able to come to a common consensus because of your similar mindsets.

Don't enter into a marriage with the expectation of changing your spouse because you can't. Committing too fast to a relationship and thinking that you can change your spouse's unfavorable behaviors will only make you miserable and risk a failed marriage.

Divorce is not a disgrace. If you value your long-term happiness, it might be the only way to mend a grave mistake committed in a relationship, albeit in a way that is costly. Forget about the social stigma around divorce because other people do not walk in your shoes.

Beyond the heartthrob and beauty, marrying a partner who thinks similarly to you will give you a lot of satisfaction later in life. The romantic thrill decays with time, but your mindset stays forever. It is better not to marry than to fail in marriage and make your children suffer.

PARENTING

YOU MAY HAVE HEARD the maxim "Spare the rod, spoil the child" when discussing how to discipline your children. It is tempting to believe that if you don't beat your children, they will grow up to be stiff-necked and recalcitrant. But it is questionable whether you can really gain your children's cooperation by hitting them.[38] Your children may comply with you temporarily because you are perceived as a threat, but they will remember the beating. They will want to stay away from you if they can. You are more likely to sever your bond with your children than anything else. In severe cases, this poor relationship with your children can be irreparable, and you may feel remorseful as you grow old without realizing that it all began with the beating. Many elderly people who are near the end of their lives have regretted having done this to their children.

Furthermore, when children are at a young age, their brains are still experiencing prime plasticity, they will learn to use aggression to solve problems and will bring this negative behavior into their adulthood. And with your children distancing themselves from you, you will have created more problems for them. They could begin to avoid adults because all adults are bad in their minds. When they grow up, they won't open up with you about their (impulsive) major life decisions. At worst, they may start to seek abusive partners. Studies also show that children who received frequent corporal punishment grew up to punish their spouse and children similarly.[39]

The risk of ruining your relationship with your kids and causing them mental harm is too high when compared to the unfounded illusion of positive effects of harsh discipline. Never believe that physical punishment is the only way to discipline children. Instead, use respectful ways to discipline your kids, such as telling them they can't play with certain toys for a week.

Sometimes the temptation to beat them can be strong when they get on your nerves. You must be strong and ignore this urge. Improve your self-control in this way, and you will keep yourself from future regret. Not having your children want to be around you in your old age makes you lose meaning and purpose in life.

If you have multiple children, you ought to avoid favoritism among them. No matter how much you want to deny it, you will prefer one child over the others. There is nothing heinous about it. One of your children just suits you better than the rest of them. The most essential thing is to conceal your favoritism, or you will risk creating sibling rivalries.

If you are wealthy, there will be the temptation to provide constant monetary gifts to your less-able adult children. You may think that you are doing the right thing and that someday your children will be independent thanks to your continued financial support. Unfortunately, the message you are sending to them is "It's okay if you don't have money. I'll always be here to support you." Your adult children, especially if they're living extravagant lifestyles, are less likely to become independent. Success can only happen to those who work their tails off, not those who count on tax-free money from their parents.

Reducing Regret

Regret can cause a lot of unhappiness for you. You may make many foolhardy decisions in your life, and that may fill your future self with regret. When you get old, it can be crucifying to learn that you made so many silly, avoidable mistakes. Reducing the likelihood of regret as much as possible will help reduce unhappiness in your future.

THINGS THAT YOU DIDN'T ENJOY

AS BANAL AS it may sound, taking time to enjoy life is an idea that is too often overlooked. The busyness of modern pursuits can make enjoyment an act of shame. You are not abandoning your future by present enjoyment. You are, in fact, planning for your future by planning what you must enjoy now. We put off too many things that we can enjoy in the present, thinking that they can wait until next time, only to realize that next time, the chance is already gone.

- The food that you liked to eat but were thrifty with is no longer accessible since you've retired to another city that does not sell it.
- The mountain that you planned to climb twenty years ago is no longer an option for your weak legs.
- The country with cold weather that you planned to visit when you got rich is no longer a possibility because of your fragile health.

We do not actively remind ourselves of the shortness of life until we get very old. Start to seize what's important to you in your daily life now, and don't wait until it is too late. This is not about squandering your money on everything you enjoy, but don't pinch your pennies so much that you sacrifice the joy of living.

Things that You Didn't Suffer

JUST AS YOU sometimes make decisions that leave your future self feeling regretful, you also make decisions that bring that self more problems.

- You neglect exercise now to create a weak body for your future self.
- You gorge on unhealthy food now to let your future self be bedridden during retirement.
- You skip education now to limit your future self's career options.

You might tend to favor instant gratification over long-term benefits. You might desire to experience pleasurable experiences now and can't stand any suffering that may be needed to fulfil your long-term goals. This can be overcome by optimizing your self-control. I detailed practical steps regarding how to maximize your willpower usage in *Peak Self-Control* if you haven't read that yet.

Things that You Didn't Do

In the long run, people feel more regretful with inaction than by making a wrong choice.[40] You feel more regretful not buying that once-in-a-lifetime cheap stock that turns out very well than to buy a stock that turns out bad. You can console yourself that you have learned from your mistake or that at least you tried, but you have nothing to use as consolation in the case of inaction.

The most regrettable inactions are ones that cost you a lot of opportunities.

- Putting off writing that book until you retire when you could've done so earlier.
- Putting off saying "I love you" to your lover, even though she loved you too but thought you didn't, so she left to be with another person.
- Putting off pursuing your business idea that turns out to be lucrative when you do try it late in life.

When you reach old age, you will likely realize that most of the reasons why you chose to put things off were silly. You realize that there is no shame in revealing your love to your sweetheart, even if she/he ends up rejecting you.

For every decision you make now, consider whether it will cause regret for your future self. There is no time like now to do your best and embrace your remaining days of life. Alas, we are often too short-sighted to think about our future selves.

Unhappiness is not your mistake. Use your realistic mindset to assess your situation and not live in false positivity. You cannot will yourself to switch on or off your happiness.

Human life is peppered with unfortunate and fortunate events. You can't escape unfortunate events to stay happy. This is life as it is. No one, including positive psychologists, can live in eternal happiness, even after applying all the popular techniques, using the most expensive happiness app, or being mindful all day long.

4

PLAN TO MAXIMIZE THE MIND'S POTENTIAL

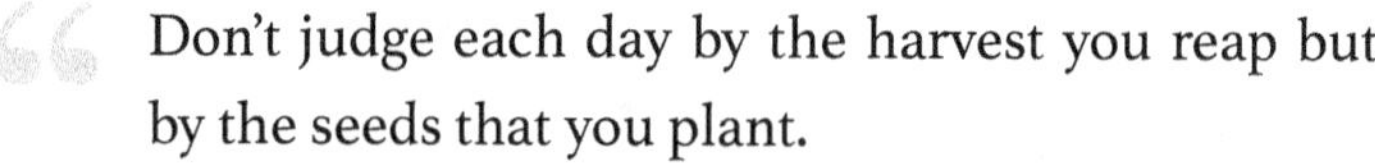

Don't judge each day by the harvest you reap but by the seeds that you plant.

— Robert Louis Stevenson

Watch for important milestones throughout your life and your children's lives to maximize the right mindset formation in them. We have learned that one misstep could snowball into long-term problems. The earlier you tackle a mindset problem, the longer you will enjoy the fruition of your hard work.

Children

Between the ages of zero and eight, a child's frontal lobe, which includes the prefrontal cortex, is not fully developed enough to think critically. The prefrontal cortex starts to develop between eight and twelve. Until then, children are amenable and easily believe what you tell them. They are also the most vulnerable to brainwashing and the instillation of negative beliefs. It is crucial that you instill positive beliefs in their subconscious minds before their logical brains mature.

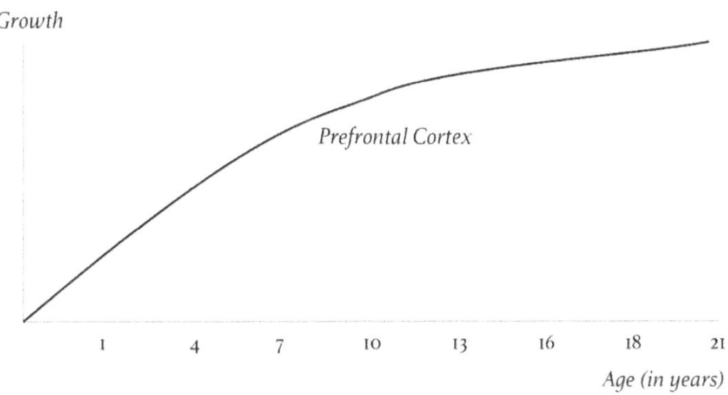

Prefrontal Cortex Development

Source: Casey et al., 2008

- Don't discourage them from their dreams—no matter how ridiculous they may sound. They may just come true.
- Being overprotective of your children does not give them the chance to solve problems on their own, causing them to struggle with coping with even small levels of stress as they grow up.
- Plant positive thoughts and a growth mindset in their brains early on to support their learning journey. Tell

them "You are improving" (growth mindset), not "You were born smart" (fixed mindset).

- Don't joke with them using destructive words or phrases such as "How stupid you are" or "Why can't you learn?" Remember that the subconscious mind does not evaluate whether messages are right or wrong. The subconscious mind accepts anything that is passed to it as fact. Be mindful, though, that these negative words may come from their friends or even siblings.

- Sincerely have high expectations for your child to elicit the Rosenthal effect. Let them pick up on your expectations and fulfil that prophecy. These high expectations can lead to high self-discipline, high integrity, and high self-motivation.

- Avoid corporal punishment to reduce your future regret.

- Starting at the age of five, introduce your children to the daily practice of gratitude journaling and self-affirmation to implant positivity in their minds.

Investing in the right mindset early on pays a lot of dividends when your children grow up because it sets in motion how they will live their lives.

ADULTS

I ASSUME you are reading this book as an adult, so I will switch the focus to you.

- If you were exposed to any negative thoughts or beliefs during your childhood, don't worry. You can still undo the impact of these by practicing the methods outlined in this book. There is no need to blame your parents, who may not have understood how the subconsciousness works.
- Choose a life partner who has a similar mindset as you over one with better looks.
- Decide on your secondary education journey based solely on your interests, not on a career's earning power.
- Be open to any opportunity. You may just find your passion as you get more involved.
- Realism trumps positivity.
- Prioritize spending your money on attaining education and achievements, not status items. Children follow what their parents do. If you always feel obligated to spend to keep up with the Joneses, your children will inevitably pick up the same mindset.

CONCLUSION

After learning that your subconsciousness can steer your life for the better or for worse, I hope you will put a deliberate effort into fertilizing it with the right messages now, for when you do, you will begin to see your life moving toward your expected goals. Use this gift to your advantage in every aspect of your life. Indeed, luck plays a vital role, but you can use your subconsciousness to increase your success rate.

Use a realistic mental attitude when facing your problems. Accept that stress will follow you to your last breath. There is no escaping it. No matter how much sunshine you strive for, you will still face unpleasant things in life. Embrace this and prepare yourself to face them. Learning to manage your stress can help you cope with life more easily.

Don't obsess over reaching happiness at the achievement of your goals; instead, strive to work on things you are good at to gain fulfillments from your work.

Having the right mindset increases your happiness and motivation, which in turn helps fuel long-haul journeys toward reaching difficult goals. You are certainly capable of achieving what you set yourself up for.

Thanks for completing this book.

KEEP IN TOUCH

If this book benefits you, would you please take a moment to write a review? I would love to read your comments. It would mean a lot to me hearing directly from readers like you.

Keep in touch with me at said@saidhasyim.com.

If you wish to be notified of my next book update or special promotion, sign up to my mailing list at https://www.saidhasyim.com.

For a limited time and while stocks last, access the bonus material at https://www.saidhasyim.com/peak-mindset-exclusive if you purchased this book.

ALSO BY SAID HASYIM

ABOUT THE AUTHOR

Said Hasyim is a certified IT project manager with an obsession for finding the best ways to maximize his productivity. After more than a decade of arduous self-experimentation and research into bio-hacks, Said discovered various methods to improve his productivity. Now, he hopes to share his findings with his readers in his *Peak Productivity* book series to unleash their inner potential.

Find out more about Said at www.saidhasyim.com.

facebook.com/SaidHasyimReal

instagram.com/SaidHasyimReal

linkedin.com/in/saidhasyim

NOTES

1. The Subconsciousness

1. Bargh, J. A., & Morsella, E. (2008). The Unconscious Mind. *Perspectives on Psychological Science: A Journal of the Association for Psychological Science, 3*(1), 73–79. https://doi.org/10.1111/j.1745-6916.2008.00064.x
2. Bargh, J. A., Chen, M., & Burrows, L. (1996). Automaticity of social behavior: Direct effects of trait construct and stereotype activation on action. *Journal of Personality and Social Psychology, 71*(2), 230–244. https://doi.org/10.1037/0022-3514.71.2.230
3. Scrutton, T. (2018). Can being told you're ill make you ill? A discussion of psychiatry, religion and out of the ordinary experiences. *Think, 17*(49), 87–101. doi:10.1017/S1477175618000131
4. Dunn, G., & Pooley, D. (2010). Belief systems as the foundation for our professional evolution. *The Journal of the Canadian Chiropractic Association, 54*(2), 76–80.
5. Phillips, D. P., Liu, G. C., Kwok, K., Jarvinen, J. R., Zhang, W., & Abramson, I. S. (2001). The Hound of the Baskervilles effect: Natural experiment on the influence of psychological stress on timing of death. *BMJ (Clinical research ed.), 323*(7327), 1443–1446. https://doi.org/10.1136/bmj.323.7327.1443
6. Oleson, K. C., Poehlmann, K. M., Yost, J. H., Lynch, M. E., & Arkin, R. M. (2000). Subjective overachievement: Individual differences in self-doubt and concern with performance. *Journal of Personality, 68*(3), 491–524. https://doi.org/10.1111/1467-6494.00104/
7. Sharot, T. (2011). The optimism bias. *Current Biology, 21*(23), R941–R945. https://doi.org/10.1016/j.cub.2011.10.030
8. Kusse, C., Shaffii-LE Bourdiec, A., Schrouff, J., Matarazzo, L., & Maquet, P. (2012). Experience-dependent induction of hypnagogic images during daytime naps: A combined behavioural and EEG study. *Journal of Sleep Research, 21*(1), 10–20. https://doi.org/10.1111/j.1365-2869.2011.00939.x/
9. Ma, K., Sellaro, R., Lippelt, D. P., & Hommel, B. (2016). Mood migration: How enfacing a smile makes you happier. *Cognition, 151*, 52–62. https://doi.org/10.1016/j.cognition.2016.02.018/

10. Anat Rafaeli, Jane Dutton, Celia V. Harquail, and Stephanie Mackie-Lewis, 1997: Navigating by attire: The use of dress by female administrative employees. *AMJ*, 40, 9–45, https://doi.org/10.5465/257019

11. Bernardi, N. F., De Buglio, M., Trimarchi, P. D., Chielli, A., & Bricolo, E. (2013). Mental practice promotes motor anticipation: Evidence from skilled music performance. *Frontiers in Human Neuroscience*, 7, 451. https://doi.org/10.3389/fnhum.2013.00451/

12. Ng B. (2018). The neuroscience of growth mindset and intrinsic motivation. *Brain Sciences*, 8(2), 20. https://doi.org/10.3390/brainsci8020020/

13. Blackwell, L. S., Trzesniewski, K. H., & Dweck, C. S. (2007). Implicit theories of intelligence predict achievement across an adolescent transition: A longitudinal study and an intervention. *Child Development*, 78(1), 246–263. https://doi.org/10.1111/j.1467-8624.2007.00995.x/

14. Dunning, D., Heath, C., & Suls, J. M. (2004). Flawed self-assessment: Implications for health, education, and the workplace. *Psychological Science in the Public Interest*, 5(3), 69–106.https://doi.org/10.1111/j.1529-1006.2004.00018.x

15. Baldwin, A. S., Kiviniemi, M. T., & Snyder, M. (2009). A subtle source of power: The effect of having an expectation on anticipated interpersonal power. *The Journal of Social Psychology*, 149(1), 82–104. https://doi.org/10.3200/SOCP.149.1.82-104

16. Rosenthal, R., Jacobson, L. Pygmalion in the classroom. *Urban Rev, 3*, 16–20 (1968). https://doi.org/10.1007/BF02322211

17. Port, D. R. (2019, December 2). Rocket Matter Announces Series on Depression, Substance Abuse, and Wellness in the Legal Community. *Rocket Matter.* https://www.rocketmatter.com/attorney-wellness/rocket-matter-announces-series-depression-substance-abuse-wellness-legal-community/

2. The Stressful Mind

1. Morey, J. N., Boggero, I. A., Scott, A. B., & Segerstrom, S. C. (2015). Current directions in stress and human immune function. *Current Opinion in Psychology, 5*, 13–17. https://doi.org/10.1016/j.copsyc.2015.03.007

2. Rodin J. (1986). Aging and health: Effects of the sense of control. *Science (New York, N.Y.), 233*(4770), 1271–1276. https://doi.org/10.1126/science.3749877

3. Koffer, R., Drewelies, J., Almeida, D. M., Conroy, D. E., Pincus, A. L., Gerstorf, D., & Ram, N. (2017). The role of general and daily control beliefs for affective stressor-reactivity across adulthood and old age. *The*

Journals of Gerontology: Series B, *74*(2), 242–253. https://doi.org/10.1093/geronb/gbx055

4. Melanie H. Mallers, PhD, Maria Claver, PhD, Lisa A. Lares, MS. (2014). Perceived control in the lives of older adults: The influence of Langer and Rodin's work on gerontological theory, policy, and practice, *The Gerontologist*, *54*(1), 67–74. https://doi.org/10.1093/geront/gnt051

5. Curtis, R., Groarke, A., & Sullivan, F. (2014). Stress and self-efficacy predict psychological adjustment at diagnosis of prostate cancer. *Scientific Reports*, *4*, 5569. https://doi.org/10.1038/srep05569

6. Center for Substance Abuse Treatment (US). (2014). *A Treatment Improvement Protocol: Trauma-Informed Care in Behavioral Health Services*, *57*, 51–89. https://www.ncbi.nlm.nih.gov/books/NBK207191

7. Farias, M., & Wikholm, C. (2016). Has the science of mindfulness lost its mind? *BJPsych Bulletin*, *40*(6), 329–332. https://doi.org/10.1192/pb.bp.116.053686

8. Kreplin, U., Farias, M. & Brazil, I.A. (2018). The limited prosocial effects of meditation: A systematic review and meta-analysis. *Sci Rep*, *8*, 2403. https://doi.org/10.1038/s41598-018-20299-z

9. Paul Grossman & Nicholas T. Van Dam. (2011). Mindfulness, by any other name…: Trials and tribulations of sati in western psychology and science, *Contemporary Buddhism*, *12*(1), 219–239, DOI:10.1080/14639947.2011.564841

10. Toneatto, T., & Nguyen, L. (2007). Does mindfulness meditation improve anxiety and mood symptoms? A review of the controlled research. *The Canadian Journal of Psychiatry*, *52*(4), 260–266. https://doi.org/10.1177/070674370705200409

11. Draganski, B., & May, A. (2008). Training-induced structural changes in the adult human brain. *Behavioural Brain Research*, *192*(1), 137–142. https://doi.org/10.1016/j.bbr.2008.02.015

12. Greene, D. J., Black, K. J., & Schlaggar, B. L. (2016). Considerations for MRI study design and implementation in pediatric and clinical populations. *Developmental Cognitive Neuroscience*, *18*, 101–112. https://doi.org/10.1016/j.dcn.2015.12.005

13. Shapiro D. H., Jr. (1992). Adverse effects of meditation: A preliminary investigation of long-term meditators. *International Journal of Psychosomatics: official publication of the International Psychosomatics Institute*, *39*(1–4), 62–67.

14. Bastir, M., Rosas, A., Gunz, P.*et al.* (2011). Evolution of the base of the brain in highly encephalized human species. *Nat Commun*, *2*, 588. https://doi.org/10.1038/ncomms1593

15. Dhammahaso, P. H. (2020). Buddhism: A Religion of Positivism or Presentism? A Study of Bhaddhekaretta Sutta. *Asia Pacific Journal of*

Religions and Cultures, *1*(2), 1–10. Retrieved from https://so06.tci-thaijo.org/index.php/ajrc/article/view/241090

16. University of Texas at Austin. (2011, March 24). Psychologists find the meaning of aggression: 'Monty Python' scene helps research. *ScienceDaily*. Retrieved April 3, 2021 from www.sciencedaily.com/releases/2011/03/110323105202.htm

17. https://www.researchgate.net/publication/47403010_Whatever_Does_Not_Kill_Us_Cumulative_Lifetime_Adversity_Vulnerability_and_Resilience

18. https://pubmed.ncbi.nlm.nih.gov/23437923/

19. https://www.ncbi.nlm.nih.gov/pmc/articles/PMC3128334/#:~:text=First%2C%20the%20undoing%20effect%20occurs,occurs%20for%20men%20as%20well

3. The Happiness Deception

1. Brickman, P., Coates, D., & Janoff-Bulman, R. (1978). Lottery winners and accident victims: Is happiness relative? *Journal of Personality and Social Psychology*, *36*(8), 917–927. https://doi.org/10.1037//0022-3514.36.8.917

2. Welles, J. F. (2018). Cognitive Dissonance Revisited. *Neuroscience and Neurological Surgery*, *2*(1), 01. https://doi.org/10.31579/2578-8868/025

3. Gerard, H. B., & Mathewson, G. C. (1966). The effect of severity of initiation on liking for a group: A replication. *Journal of Experimental Social Psychology*, *2*(3), 278–287. https://doi.org/10.1016/0022-1031(66)90084-9

4. Lyubomirsky, S., King, L., & Diener, E. (2005). The benefits of frequent positive affect: does happiness lead to success? *Psychological Bulletin*, *131*(6), 803–855. https://doi.org/10.1037/0033-2909.131.6.803

5. Peiró, J. M., Kozusznik, M. W., Rodríguez-Molina, I., & Tordera, N. (2019). The happy-productive worker model and beyond: Patterns of wellbeing and performance at work. *International Journal of Environmental Research and Public Health*, *16*(3), 479. https://doi.org/10.3390/ijerph16030479

6. Association for Psychological Science. (2008, March 6). Genes Hold The Key To How Happy We Are, Scientists Say. *ScienceDaily*. Retrieved April 4, 2021 from www.sciencedaily.com/releases/2008/03/080304103308.htm

7. Dubol, M. et al. (2018). Dopamine transporter and reward anticipation in a dimensional perspective: A multimodal brain imaging study. *Neuropsychopharmacology: official publication of the American College of Neuropsychopharmacology*, *43*(4), 820–827. https://doi.org/10.1038/npp.2017.183

8. Arntz, A., Van Eck, M., & de Jong, P. J. (1992). Unpredictable sudden increases in intensity of pain and acquired fear. *Journal of Psychophysiology, 6*(1), 54–64.

9. Hu, J., & Hirsh, J. B. (2017). Accepting lower salaries for meaningful work. *Frontiers in Psychology, 8,* 1649. https://doi.org/10.3389/fpsyg.2017.01649

10. https://www.researchgate.net/publication/281424792_Using_signature_strengths_in_pursuit_of_goals_Effects_on_goal_progress_need_satisfaction_and_well-being_and_implications_for_coaching_psychologists

11. Moeini, B., Barati, M., Farhadian, M., & Ara, M. H. (2018). The association between social support and happiness among elderly in Iran. *Korean Journal of Family Medicine, 39*(4), 260–265. https://doi.org/10.4082/kjfm.17.0121

12. Chou, A. F., Stewart, S. L., Wild, R. C., & Bloom, J. R. (2012). Social support and survival in young women with breast carcinoma. *Psycho-Oncology, 21*(2), 125–133. https://doi.org/10.1002/pon.1863

13. Wang, X., Cai, L., Qian, J., & Peng, J. (2014). Social support moderates stress effects on depression. *International Journal of Mental Health Systems, 8*(1), 41. https://doi.org/10.1186/1752-4458-8-41

14. Compare, A. et al. (2013). Social support, depression, and heart disease: a ten year literature review. *Frontiers in Psychology, 4,* 384. https://doi.org/10.3389/fpsyg.2013.00384

15. Ozbay, F., Johnson, D. C., Dimoulas, E., Morgan, C. A., Charney, D., & Southwick, S. (2007). Social support and resilience to stress: from neurobiology to clinical practice. *Psychiatry (Edgmont (Pa.: Township)), 4*(5), 35–40.

16. Heggie B. A. (2019). The healing power of laughter. *Journal of Hospital Medicine, 14*(5), 320. https://doi.org/10.12788/jhm.3205

17. Mathers, N. (2016). Compassion and the science of kindness: Harvard Davis Lecture 2015. *The British Journal of General Practice: The Journal of the Royal College of General Practitioners, 66*(648), e525–e527. https://doi.org/10.3399/bjgp16X686041

18. University of Turku. (2017, June 1). Social laughter releases endorphins in the brain. *ScienceDaily.* Retrieved March 13, 2021 from www.sciencedaily.com/releases/2017/06/170601124121.htm

19. Dunbar, R. I. M., et al. (2011). Social laughter is correlated with an elevated pain threshold. *Proceedings of the Royal Society B: Biological Sciences, 279*(1731), 1161–1167. https://doi.org/10.1098/rspb.2011.1373

20. Flora, R., Zulkarnain, M., & Sukirno. (2020). β-endorphin response to aerobic and anaerobic exercises in Wistar male rats. *Medical Journal of Indonesia, 29*(3), 245–249. https://doi.org/10.13181/mji.oa.203569

21. Radosevich, P. M., Nash, J. A., Lacy, D. B., O'Donovan, C., Williams, P. E., & Abumrad, N. N. (1989). Effects of low- and high-intensity exercise on plasma and cerebrospinal fluid levels of ir-beta-endorphin, ACTH, cortisol, norepinephrine and glucose in the conscious dog. *Brain Research*, 498(1), 89–98. https://doi.org/10.1016/0006-8993(89)90402-2

22. University of Turku. (2017, August 24). HIIT releases endorphins in the brain. *ScienceDaily*. Retrieved March 6, 2021 from www.sciencedaily.com/releases/2017/08/170824101759.htm

23. Rahkila, P., Hakala, E., Alén, M., Salminen, K., & Laatikainen, T. (1988). β-Endorphin and corticotropin release is dependent on a threshold intensity of running exercise in male endurance athletes. *Life Sciences*, 43(6), 551–558. https://doi.org/10.1016/0024-3205(88)90158-0

24. University of Turku. (2017, August 28). Eating triggers endorphin release in the brain. *ScienceDaily*. Retrieved March 20, 2021 from www.sciencedaily.com/releases/2017/08/170828102719.htm

25. Lee, J. S., Kim, S. G., Kim, H. K., Baek, S. Y., & Kim, C. M. (2012). Acute effects of capsaicin on proopioimelanocortin mRNA levels in the arcuate nucleus of Sprague-Dawley rats. *Psychiatry investigation*, 9(2), 187–190. https://doi.org/10.4306/pi.2012.9.2.187

26. Holden, R., & Holden, J. (2013). Music: A better alternative than pain? *The British Journal of General Practice: the Journal of the Royal College of General Practitioners*, 63(615), 536. https://doi.org/10.3399/bjgp13X673748

27. Gerra, G. et al. (1998). Neuroendocrine responses of healthy volunteers to 'techno-music': Relationships with personality traits and emotional state. *International Journal of Psychophysiology: official journal of the International Organization of Psychophysiology*, 28(1), 99–111. https://doi.org/10.1016/s0167-8760(97)00071-8

28. Stewart, J., Garrido, S., Hense, C., & McFerran, K. (2019). Music use for mood regulation: Self-awareness and conscious listening choices in young people with tendencies to depression. *Frontiers in Psychology, 10*, 1199. https://doi.org/10.3389/fpsyg.2019.01199

29. Sachs, M. E., Damasio, A., & Habibi, A. (2015). The pleasures of sad music: A systematic review. *Frontiers in Human Neuroscience, 9*, 404. https://doi.org/10.3389/fnhum.2015.00404

30. Fredrickson, B. L., & Losada, M. F. (2005). Positive affect and the complex dynamics of human flourishing. *The American Psychologist, 60*(7), 678–686. https://doi.org/10.1037/0003-066X.60.7.678

31. Kahneman, D., & Deaton, A. (2010). High income improves evaluation of life but not emotional well-being. *Proceedings of the National Academy of Sciences, 107*(38), 16489–16493. https://doi.org/10.1073/pnas.1011492107

32. Jebb, A. T., Tay, L., Diener, E., & Oishi, S. (2018). Happiness, income satiation and turning points around the world. *Nature Human Behaviour*, 2(1), 33–38. https://doi.org/10.1038/s41562-017-0277-0

33. Ariyabuddhiphongs, V. (2010). Lottery Gambling: A Review. *Journal of Gambling Studies*, 27(1), 15–33. https://doi.org/10.1007/s10899-010-9194-0

34. Yarritu, I., Matute, H., & Vadillo, M. A. (2014). Illusion of control: The role of personal involvement. *Experimental Psychology*, 61(1), 38–47. https://doi.org/10.1027/1618-3169/a000225

35. Medvec, V. H., Madey, S. F., & Gilovich, T. (1995). When less is more: Counterfactual thinking and satisfaction among Olympic medalists. *Journal of Personality and Social Psychology*, 69(4), 603–610. https://doi.org/10.1037//0022-3514.69.4.603

36. Tummers, L., Steijn, B., Nevicka, B., & Heerema, M. (2018). The effects of leadership and job autonomy on vitality: Survey and experimental evidence. *Review of Public Personnel Administration*, 38(3), 355–377. https://doi.org/10.1177/0734371X16671980/

37. Laubu, C., Dechaume-Moncharmont, F. X., Motreuil, S., & Schweitzer, C. (2016). Mismatched partners that achieve postpairing behavioral similarity improve their reproductive success. *Science Advances*, 2(3), e1501013. https://doi.org/10.1126/sciadv.1501013

38. Bassam, E., Marianne, T. B., Rabbaa, L. K., & Gerbaka, B. (2018). Corporal punishment of children: Discipline or abuse? *The Libyan Journal of Medicine*, 13(1), 1485456. https://doi.org/10.1080/19932820.2018.1485456/

39. Gershoff, E. T., & Grogan-Kaylor, A. (2016). Spanking and child outcomes: Old controversies and new meta-analyses. *Journal of Family Psychology*, 30(4), 453–469. https://doi.org/10.1037/fam0000191

40. Gilovich, T., Wang, R. F., Regan, D., & Nishina, S. (2003). Regrets of action and inaction across cultures. *Journal of Cross-Cultural Psychology*, 34(1), 61–71. https://doi.org/10.1177/0022022102239155